NOT
FORSAKEN

NOT
FORSAKEN

GROWING UP BLACK, MALE, AND
CHRISTIAN IN THE HOOD

CHRIS McNAIR

Abingdon Press / Nashville

NOT FORSAKEN

Growing Up Black, Male, and Christian in the Hood

Library of Congress Control Number: 2021930356

ISBN 13: 978-1-7910-0000-4

ePub ISBN 978-1-7910-0001-1

21 22 23 24 25 26 27 28 29 30—10 9 8 7 6 5 4 3 2 1
MANUFACTURED IN THE UNITED STATES OF AMERICA

CONTENTS

PREFACE

Imagine You Are a Black Male Teen in North Minneapolis

By Marcus Hunter II

Star Tribune, Opinion Exchange, October 12, 2020

Imagine being looked down upon by your society as the aggressor in every situation.

Imagine not being able to step outside of your home without feeling as if you have a target on your back, fearing that you will be shot where you stand.

Imagine that every time you walk down the street in a city you call home, you are constantly and anxiously looking over your shoulder, wondering if the next couple steps you take will be your last.

I am a 17-year-old, African American man with ambition and a determination to be heard and to stand up for his Black brothers and sisters collectively. This is our reality every day in the United States of America.

Imagine watching the news or monitoring social media and seeing somebody who looks just like you being killed. You know that could be you in a body bag.

Imagine watching your Black brothers and sisters being dehumanized in unimaginable ways, slammed onto the street by the police, covered in blood, pleading for mercy. This is your so-called protection, law enforcement, that you depend on for safety.

Imagine feeling like the whole world is against your prosperity and facing constant reminders that you will never succeed in life.

Picture the following: You're walking down the street of your own neighborhood headed to the gas station or grocery store. You are not bothering anyone and your only focus is getting to your destination. You come across a group of Black men at a stop sign on the way to the store.

As you are walking toward them they stare you down intently. You are stopped. One of them comes forward and asks you, "Who you with, what's yo' set."

You have no response. Nervousness and fear kick in. You do not have an answer to give to the man questioning you.

"I'm not with all that," you say.

Moments like those drown your mind and consciousness in a pool of fear, scarring you emotionally. Giving the wrong answer in moments like these can cost you your human dignity, or your life.

Going to school as an African American male is a very different experience in today's society. I come from a family in which the highest academic achievement is a high school diploma. So there was not much discussion of an educational future.

Growing up, I've used academic achievement and accolades, working toward success—"making it out" and using school as an outlet to escape the struggle and adversity I face every day. We are faced with the reality of our Blackness and what comes with it on many occasions.

I am grateful for the rare opportunity to attend a private high school. But, in that context, I feel very different from my peers, especially coming from the experience of poverty throughout my childhood. I have a constant feeling that I am alone and that I do not belong. I was not granted the same tools and opportunities that people who do not look like me were given. It's made me feel very different from those around me. I've felt excluded from certain conversations because of the experiences that I missed out on due to the disadvantages that come with being Black and poor.

I face the constant reminder that I am not good enough to live a life in

America. To be Black is emotionally and mentally draining on levels that are unexplainable. We are in a so-called "free society," where I have never truly experienced freedom. I do not feel free. I do not know what freedom is. I am afraid of the world I live in, afraid of what will happen to me tomorrow. Every day I wake up to these thoughts and I go to sleep with them.

It angers me that I have younger cousins who have to experience constant gunshots in my North Side neighborhood. It angers me that they will have to go through the same process of experiencing the weight of their Blackness.

These are things that run through my mind constantly. These are things that are a part of me. I cannot escape. How can you ever get a break when you feel like your race is being hunted and you feel like a target is on your back every time you step out into the world?

Imagine all of these things; imagine it was your reality.

Marcus Hunter II lives in Minneapolis.

Used by permission.

INTRODUCTION

I was making a visit to the home of a family who had just been victimized by street violence. Their oldest son was shot and killed hours before in the street—apparently, a drug deal gone bad. But the family did not care about the particulars. All they knew was that their oldest and cherished boy was gone, taken from them unnecessarily, through street violence. I was there to minister to the family and talk to the father about taking his youngest son with me on a previously planned camping trip. In spite of what had happened, this child desperately needed to get out of the city for a bit.

The front yard and rooms of the home were crowded with mourners, most of them dulling their pain and grief with alcohol or marijuana. Two young men stood at the front door like sentries. They glared at me as I entered the house. I had to walk through this menacing gauntlet of mourners to conduct my visit. When I greeted the father he collapsed into my arms, crying. I spent some time with him in consolation and prayer. With the father's blessing, I left with his youngest son, whose eyes were wide with shock and grief. The funeral would be held after our return. As I exited, those who had given me menacing stares upon my arrival now greeted me with respect. I would never have gotten past the sidewalk crowd except for the grace afforded me by those who knew me as a pastor, coach, and friend from years of ministry, cultivating relationships.

Unfortunately this is not an uncommon scenario among urban Black communities. It seems like our young men have been singled out for destruction. The dearth of young Black men in the upper echelons of American society, in the political, business, and academic realms as compared to their overwhelming representation in prison, poverty, and violence in America strikes one as a genocidal plague. This prevailing trend among young Black men has deeply affected one of my friends, whom I had first met when he was a teenager. He has emerged from the quagmire of life in the inner city as a Black child to become a strong Black man—a husband, father, and a gainfully employed professional, a staple of his community. Having personally experienced the magnitude of the hazards of being young, Black, and male in urban America and witnessing the ongoing decimation of Black manhood in our society as an adult (gang violence, police brutality and killings, institutional injustice), he has come to the stark conclusion that God has forsaken young Black men. The condition facing Black men in America has caused him to fundamentally doubt the existence of a loving, just God. As a Black man I share the feelings of grief, disappointment, and rage when I consider the lives and prospects of the youth I work with, but I cannot come to the same conclusion. I see God standing on the side of oppressed Black youth. I see Jesus carrying his cross for the sake of the redemption of young Black men. Yes, we suffer; but Christ suffered before us. Christ suffers with us. He bore the wounds of injustice in his suffering and passion, for those of the whole world and for those of young Black men in the city. God is not indifferent to our suffering; on the contrary, we are enabled to draw closer to him through it. "Now, it is commendable if, because of one's understanding of God, someone should endure pain through suffering unjustly" (1 Peter 2:19). I see Christ as being the vindication, salvation, and glory of all Black people as he shows us the way to redemption and glory; promise for this world and yes, the one to come. God has not forsaken young Black men. In Christ he has identified with their struggle and in Christ he offers them life. Not just in eternity, but abundant life to be experienced and lived in the here and now. But a requisite to this life, this joy, this purpose is to come out of the world and stand in Christ. Only then can we overcome the evils of institutional sin, injustice, and oppression to be who God created us to be.

Displayed in the chapel of a hospital in Lexington, Kentucky, is a plaque with this anonymous quotation:

If people are to learn of a living and loving God
it will be through personal relationships. I realize that as
a Christian, God will use my relationships with people
to reveal Himself to them.

This sentiment has always stayed with me and has become my modus operandi for doing ministry. Building authentic and genuine relationships with urban youth takes time, but it is critical in order to be effective. Throughout my years of growth and being involved in urban areas, the Lord has allowed me to develop a certain expertise in ministering to African American male youth. This simply means that I've made plenty of mistakes, but I've stuck around long enough to learn from them. Building lasting relationships has allowed me to attain my primary goal in ministry: for young Black males in the inner city to discover Christ so that they may build lives of fulfillment, knowing that God is with them. God has not forsaken them.

MY STORY

Growing up, I was always a good kid, never got into trouble; my mom raised us in the Church and to be God-fearing. My dad was in the army and we moved around a lot, but we always attended chapel on the army base. Even though we lived in some rough neighborhoods I never got in with the wrong crowd. My big brother, Tyrone, was one of the leaders among neighborhood youth. He had a rep for being tough and all the kids in the neighborhood respected him. That worked to my advantage, helping me to negotiate the rough streets. Everyone knew I was his little brother so nobody messed with me. Tyrone was a great big brother and I looked up to him, but eventually he succumbed to the various stresses all Black boys in the city face, and we lost him to drugs. In the sixth grade, my Sunday school teachers gave me a Bible. That is my first memory of having a personal interest in God.

What I remember most before committing my life to Christ was that I worried a lot. I worried about the well-being of my mom and dad, my brothers and sisters. I worried about my classes and doing well at school. I worried about my neighborhood, about bullies and gangs and having to fight. I was quiet and shy and afraid.

When I was thirteen, my family was living in El Paso, Texas, and there we attended a United Methodist church. It was a typical small church, kind of boring but with an inviting community. It was multicultural with several Black families. In Sunday school I met Mrs. Luke, an older Black woman; she was also the youth worker. I thought, "How is this old lady supposed to get me interested in being a Christian?" She was everything the supposedly ideal youth worker is not. She was not young, not charismatic, not hip or cool. She was poor, not physically attractive or active; in fact, she had a hump in her back. Her physical deformity put me off the first time I saw her. Yet, God used her to get ahold of me *and* others like me. She made me understand that my knowledge of and relationship with God was of paramount importance—to her and to God. She imparted this understanding by being my friend. Not being cool, right, or legalistic. But by being present. Our one year together in that church started me on a life of discipleship. From her, I learned what it means to follow God and be a disciple of Christ.

People often think that to do effective ministry with urban youth, they have to look and act like them. They feel God can't use them unless they have the same ethnicity, use hip hop slang and dress, and so on. By trying to be something they are not, they fool no one, and are not being real. Mrs. Luke was simply authentic and real. I learned that to be used by God, one only needs to yield and submit to God's will. If we are where God wants us to be, God will use us. Influencing young people to follow Christ as a vocation is the most fulfilling form of service of which I can conceive. For thirty years, I've worked with urban youth as a pastor, coach, counselor, and teacher, but mostly as a friend.

CHRIST'S CHILDREN MINISTRIES

My wife, Lisa, and I began Christ's Children Ministries as a grassroots organization twenty-five years ago. My tenure as a pastor at a local church in Minneapolis had come to an end and we desired to pursue our call to minister in the community of which we had become a part.

- Our mission is to build Christian community among the unchurched children, youth, and families where we live. We do this through outreach programs with children and providing pastoral care and support for their families.
- Our philosophy is that for people to learn about a living, loving God, it will be through genuine, authentic relationship.
- Our core characteristic for doing ministry is to be incarnational; allowing Christ to be manifest in our neighborhood and community through our lives, presence, and relationships.
- Our programs are vehicles by which we facilitate and build those relationships.
- Our strategy is to use those programming contacts with children as a springboard to engender long-lasting relationships with youth and families that will become a catalyst for communal change.
- Our vision is to transform our community, seeking to influence families and neighborhoods for Christ over a long period of time, to build a sense of communal connection that will empower individuals and families to overcome many of the problems that plague us.

Christ's Children Ministries is a grassroots, nonprofit organization. We are the Church for those who have no church. We want to build Christian community among those who have no sense of connection with or responsibility to others through building relationships in Christ. Lisa and I lead the ministry. I am the executive director and pastor and she is the associate director. We have seasonally paid staff for sports and summer activities, and are joined by a small group of adult volunteers who share our vision. These are composed of young men and women who have grown up in this ministry, in relationship with us, and want to join in the work. For example, there is Tyler, who came to us seventeen years ago as a little boy and never left. He is now a college graduate, who in his spare time from his white-collar job runs our basketball program. And there's Anton who, as a little boy thirty years ago, followed me around everywhere. Not only is he a respected community leader, a licensed electrician, husband, and father, but he also provides leadership on our board of directors.

It is part of our ministry philosophy to build relationships and networks with agencies and institutions as well as people. We perceive that our community does not need more institutional buildings but connection and cooperation of agencies through sharing resources to work together. We have no permanent building in which we meet. However, through relationships forged over years and years, we have access to and use of space at local churches, schools, parks, and other local agencies to carry out the ministry activities that serve our population. Space for worship, weddings, funerals, tutoring, sports events and practices, and whatever we have going on is provided when we need it through our community network.

The legitimacy of our ministry flows from our long-term commitment to strengthening children, youth, and families in our inner-city Minneapolis community as we invite them into Christian discipleship. My wife and I live there to share community in every way with our neighbors. Our children went to school with their children. I volunteer at local schools and parks, I'm present in the neighborhood and in their lives. We see them every day. We know the ones who are at-risk and we build a sense of connection and belonging with shared experiences like sports teams, communal family dinners, house church gatherings, field trips, and retreats. Our main venue for interacting with youth is not in church but on the streets, at the parks and gyms, at school, and at home. Through age-appropriate programming, we offer pastoral care and support for the entire family. We accomplish our mission by tracking them from childhood through young adulthood, providing long-term communal support for their development, whereby they may be equipped spiritually, socially, emotionally, and mentally to succeed in life. We build relationships with children, which in many cases last their whole lives.

Our work goes beyond traditional one-on-one mentoring. Beginning at the elementary level, we engage children through discipleship and support groups. We visit children's homes, 90 percent of which have no fathers present, develop friendships with parental figures, visit schools, work with teachers and school personnel, and advocate for family needs. We offer long-term relationships that help create a network of support and encouragement through counseling, advocacy, and our house church, which extends to the whole family. There are many program activities, but the strength of our ministry is in consistent relationship.

There have been times when the long years of struggling and laboring in relationships seemed to yield no visible fruit. Yet, we never lost sight that this is God's work, and God is faithful. In some families we are now seeing the third generation of our influence for Christ grow up here. Men, who began with us as boys, are now raising children of their own. Men, who were teens when I coaxed them out of the street life, are now influencing young people around them as fathers, teachers, and husbands.

MY HOOD

When I first arrived, I looked around and thought, "This is the inner city?!" I had served in very run-down and impoverished neighborhoods in Lexington, Kentucky. I had spent time on Chicago's West Side with the blocks of dilapidated and abandoned apartment buildings and houses. I once visited Compton, California, with its gangs and drug dealing. While inner-city Minneapolis looked like none of these places, not nearly as physically intimidating or obviously threatening, it was every bit as devastated an area. It did not have the magnitude of larger cities but the debilitating quality of the suffering was the same, with *all* the elements of urban decay. I soon learned that more than physical surroundings were the issues of despondency and despair in the hearts and minds of people. People suffer and endure the same pain, whether in the upper Midwest or on the crowded East or West Coast. A child, dead from a stray bullet from a shot fired by gang violence, is just as dead in North Minneapolis as in Compton. The ravages of poverty and the effect of social estrangement may have lived behind closed doors and lain beneath the notice of casual passersby on the near North Side, and yet they were there in full force.

The demographics of our neighborhood are diverse: 55 percent Black, 17 percent Asian American, 14 percent White, 9 percent Hispanic, and 5 percent other ethnicities. Fifty-eight percent of households live at or below the poverty level. Close to 40 percent of families are single-parent households.[1] The local school is our primary source of contact with youth. Eighty percent of its students are African American and 93 percent qualify for the free/reduced lunch program. It has the lowest academic scores in Minnesota, a state whose education achievement gap is among the worst in the nation.[2] To me, this is the clearest indicator of the crisis of poverty among these children.

Education is the building block, the primary step for advancement and self-sufficiency in our society. An entire generation of Black children here are growing up without this basic staple necessary for subsistence in American society. We, the generation that most benefited from increased educational opportunities for Black people from *Brown v. the Board of Education* [of Topeka, 1954] to the Affirmative Action legislation of the 1960s–'70s, are watching the hopes and dreams of a generation of children being aborted before our eyes for lack of basic skills to which they are entitled as American citizens. As a society, we are sowing the seeds of our own destruction fomenting social dysfunction and crisis that will impact the nation and world. Because of this, I spend a significant amount of time volunteering in classrooms in addition to conducting twice-weekly mentoring groups for boys.

Christ's Children Ministries targets African American boys because we believe that this is how we can have the most lasting impact for change. The behavior of Black boys is at the root of most urban problems, manifesting in crime, gangs, drugs, and violence. We believe that if we can influence boys and affect their outlook on life, entire families will be transformed. We feel that if we can lift up their self-esteem and self-awareness, instill hope, and build character, we will elevate entire communities. Strong and secure Black boys become strong men: husbands, fathers, and uncles. They have the ability to become leaders at home and in their neighborhoods, who influence not only their immediate surroundings but society as a whole.

The vast majority of the boys who interact with our ministry have no father at home. They are at risk of falling prey to the whole gamut of negative trends facing inner-city Black youth today: joining gangs, committing crimes, dropping out of school. We have found that children often do not benefit from available support services for poor children and families because participation in those services requires the active and attentive involvement of an adult in the children's lives, which too many do not have. Many times so much effort and time go into negotiating those services that families are further stressed and exhausted, and children's needs for positive social engagement and development are overlooked. Single moms, who are struggling to meet the basic needs of their children, may be unable to get as involved in their child's education as they would like, get their child in that after-school program, or have the resources to provide transportation to sporting events or activities. The children who gravitate to our ministry are those who do not have anyone advocating for them to receive help for educational, social, physical, and/or spiritual engagement and development.

WORKING WITH BLACK YOUTH IN THE CITY

We've learned that the vast majority of Black male youth in the hood may be at-risk but are not yet street. Too many people in mainstream society are instinctively afraid of them, but most are decent kids who must navigate a vast gray area between being socially safe and acceptable and being dangerous or self-destructive. There is a significant difference in urban culture between being "straight" or "street." *Street* means a child or youth is in a lifestyle that includes gangs, drugs, crime, and everything that comes with it. Street means the person is on the way to becoming a thug or gangbanger, mostly associating with others who also feel left out and ostracized from mainstream society. This group becomes family, not the traditional settings such as school, sports, or home. This young man feels like he doesn't fit in anywhere else; the gang is the group of people with whom he now feels a sense of connection. The street lifestyle is countercultural to mainstream society.

Straight folks, on the other hand, consider themselves part of mainstream culture, sharing similar values and mores despite being poor. Although their culture may reflect a different outlook on society and reflect differing standards, they share essentially the same aspirations and hopes for themselves and their children as middle-class families. They try to live morally and socially decent lives. Many of the youth may have associations with gangs, necessary to survive in some of their neighborhoods, but in reality are not wholly into the gang culture. While the majority of youth in the inner city are not deeply involved in the crime, violence, and drug abuse plaguing their communities, they are surrounded by it constantly and influenced by the lure of peer pressure to belong. Random violence, survival strategies, and social ostracization create a reality for them that is alien to mainstream society.

> ## The best solution for the struggles that plague young people in the city is preventative action.

The violence is random because there is no pattern. We used to tell kids that if you stay off the streets at night, avoid bad places, and refrain from hanging with certain people, then violence will not find you. The truth is, it can happen anywhere, at any time. Children are killed by stray bullets that come through the walls of their homes. A person can be responsible, take precautions, and make good choices, but in this neighborhood if you are Black and poor, violence can find you.

The best solution for the struggles that plague young people in the city is preventative action. Therefore the principles of ministry expounded upon in this book target vulnerable young Black males. Our goal is to assist youth workers to help children and youth grow and develop toward maturity and self-sufficiency and be equipped with the tools required to succeed in life. To that end we have provided examples, stories, and models of education, experiences, and socialization. To paraphrase the apostle Paul, while worldly training is of some value, godliness has value for all things. "It has promise for this life now and the life to come" (1 Timothy 4:8). In order to not just survive, but thrive in their environments, urban Black male youth need to be equipped not only with academic and social skills but also with spiritual knowledge and strength. They need to come to a realization of who they are in Christ. If this is achieved, urban Black male youth may aspire to and work toward their God-given potential as productive members and leaders of society. This realization requires the instilling of certain core values. It is those values that you will read about in the following chapters of this book.

Chapter One: The Color of God

Christianity often asserts that God is colorless and color-blind. Yet, from stained glass windows to contemporary images of Christ to the values expounded from pulpits, the evidence is a prevailing understanding that God is White. The fact is, the experience of most Black people in American society is predicated on the color of their skin. What does it mean to be made in God's image if you are Black? If you are Black, is God blind or irrelevant to your struggle? *Sankofa*, a Swahili phrase, is loosely translated: "If you don't know where you came from how can you know where you are going?" In discipling urban Black male youth, it is critical for leaders to help youth find a point of identification with their Creator God, from which they come. In our program and in the chapter, we teach that God is not color-blind; God is the essence of all cultures. We have found that a positive conviction concerning their God-given Blackness can prevent many youth from falling prey to systemic racism or to the pressure of emulating negative and immoral stereotypes of Black men abundant in our society.

Chapter Two: Becoming a Man

At the core of the struggle of urban Black male youth are their aspirations to manhood. How does a young person in the inner city learn what it means to be a man if there is no one there to teach him? Black male youth in the city need to see alternatives to the negative and self-destructive lifestyles that are modeled and even glorified in many urban communities as well as in the media. Who decides when a young boy becomes a man? What are the criteria for manhood? How will boys know what they want to be as men unless they learn what they can be? This chapter offers some answers to these questions and alternate models of aspiration for Black urban male youth.

Chapter Three: A Godly Man

Ideally, values of knowing the difference between right and wrong (ethics and morality) are acquired as children grow up and mature in the bosom of their families. The prevailing drive among the urban poor is that of survival; ethics and morality often come second to figuring out how you will eat, where you will sleep, or how to avoid violence, harassment, and/or unwarranted police attention. Under these conditions, it is hard to define a moral absolute. Indeed, standards of morality are defined by the ethics of survival. Yet God's

Word posits that there is a moral absolute, a standard that is based in Christ, a guide to living life with a clean conscience, regardless of the urban, social, and moral decay that imbue everyday circumstances. This chapter outlines a guide that is not dictated by the social mores of mainstream society but by God's Word and the life of Jesus Christ, who must be the model of godliness and manliness for urban young men.

Chapter Four: A Christian in the Hood

Effective discipleship takes into account cultural context, which for young urban Black males includes peers, home, and relationships. The peer group—that is, other Black males in the hood—is the defining source of community and dramatically influences values, dress, conduct, and choices. Family and home environment also define young people's outlook on life and view of the world. Family dysfunction induced by chemical and/or physical abuse, financial problems, and/or the lack of basic needs being met induces a state of stress and despair and a sense of estrangement, which fundamentally impacts how they view and interact with mainstream society. This estrangement is most manifested in interpersonal relationships at home, at school, and in the workplace producing low self-esteem and image, an inability to trust, and emotional detachment. This chapter will help leaders understand how having an identity in Christ equips young Black boys and men with the positive self-image and esteem necessary to overcome the emotional and social perils of their environment.

Chapter Five: Just Wanna Be Happy

Happiness is experiencing personal satisfaction and fulfillment with one's life. Everyone wants to be happy: at peace, stress-free, and materially, socially, and emotionally comfortable. Happiness often eludes those who are caught in cycles of dysfunction and systematic oppressions beyond their control. In a capitalistic, Western society, happiness can be perceived as being only for the privileged and not for the poor. Without wealth and possessions how can the poor be happy? This chapter will help leaders communicate that true satisfaction and fulfillment come through relationship with God through Christ. Happiness is not the sole province of the rich or middle class; those who are poor and oppressed can attain peace and fulfillment as well. Communion with God yields peace, security, and fulfillment, even in the midst of the most trying circumstances. Obedience to God and hope in Christ lead to joy, which, unlike happiness, is not dependent on one's external circumstances. Hope is what urban Black male youth need to be happy, fulfilled, and at peace—the hope that comes through knowing who you are in Christ.

Chapter Six: "I Want to Get Paid!"

Everyone on the face on the earth wants to be valued and appreciated. However, in a world of conspicuous consumption, wherein bigger houses, cars, and wealth connote importance in society, it is hard for young people to find legitimate, social affirmation. Urban Black male youth want bigger and better everything too! They want to be noticed and recognized as unique. The means of gaining wealth and the trappings of success is not important. Acceptance, vindication, and legitimacy are the goal. Often the immediate means is a self-destructive path of crime, gangs, and early paternity that may lead to communal affirmation but also to community degradation. This chapter will help leaders teach young men how to meet the need for affirmation in positive and life-fulfilling ways: through education, hard work, and positive conduct, means which yield long-term reward.

Chapter Seven: Fitting In

The majority of urban Black male youth are not the gangbangers, drug dealers, and criminals often portrayed in the media. They are just young people trying to find out where they fit in or belong. Life in the inner city does daily damage to their concept of who they are and who they want to be. The struggle for survival, to have immediate physical needs met, often overshadows deep emotional needs. As a result, the whole of society suffers because we fail to meet the needs of our children. In order to fit in with their immediate urban community, Black boys may be called upon to engage in socially unacceptable behavior, but they do not fit in with mainstream society because due to socioeconomic factors they themselves are often deemed unacceptable. Many times the ability to avoid trouble in the neighborhood depends on familiarity with the ways of the street. Immersed in a culture of ghetto behavior whether that is truly how they see themselves or not, how do urban Black male youth meet the need to fit in while daily engaged in a struggle to survive? In this chapter, we offer guidance to a deeper community in Christ where they can be who God created them to be.

Chapter Eight: Being Black

An understanding of Blackness is first drawn from experience in the home and community. Blackness in the contemporary ghetto is only one part of the Black experience. You can't fully know what it means to be Black if all you know is the ghetto. In many cities, much of the Black population is found in center-city neighborhoods, typically low-income areas. Youth must be provided with experiences and models of Blackness that extend beyond their immediate community. They must be exposed to the richness of African American heritage, the strength of Black culture, and the deep spirituality of Black people so that they may become secure in their Blackness and not adhere to the negative stereotypes acted out around them. In this chapter, we look at ways for young people to develop an accurate self-image; to embrace, learn, and experience what it truly means to be Black; and to become secure in their Blackness.

Chapter Nine: In Christ

In this final chapter, I describe my vision for men and boys growing up in the hood, a vision that is grounded in the apostle Paul's letter to the Ephesians. Through an exploration of Ephesians, I show how Black men and boys can come to know that they belong to the Lord, realizing that they are in Christ, and Christ is in them. Through Christ, they can attain to the splendor and glory of who they are meant to be as children of God. They need Christ to be authentically Black, authentically male, and to achieve success and satisfaction in life.

CONCLUSION

"My God, my God, why have you forsaken me?" (Matthew 27:46 NIV) was Jesus's cry on the cross. He was at the point of physical and spiritual death on the cross, taking on the sins of the world, the sin that separates all from God. He felt utterly alone and forsaken, disconnected from the love, strength, and security of relationship with God the Father. But was he truly alone? God never forsakes and is indeed even more present in the most dire circumstance. Despite how he felt, the Crucifixion event was part of a larger, wonderful plan to restore humankind to fellowship with God.

Like Jesus on the cross, many African American male youth in the city feel forsaken by God. They are cheated by the promise of the American dream, effectively cut off from social success due to the invisible barriers of socioeconomic conditions, racism, and both personal and social dysfunction. Young Black men feel endangered, even hunted by society. Many are literally living in fear for their lives because of violence and crime in the neighborhood. Disproportionately high incarceration, murder, and addiction rates take their toll. They ask, "Is this life? Is this all there is?" They may doubt the existence of God and ask: "Where is God? Has God forsaken *me*?" But God has not forsaken African American male youth in the hood. On the contrary, God has uniquely positioned them for leadership in the community, in society, and among the people of God.

Over the years, I have been asked at different times, usually after having to face some communal crisis such as a shooting death or sentence of imprisonment for the loved one of a family: "Do you feel like you are a success?" "Do you feel like you've made a difference?" I'm not here to be a success by temporal definitions. I'm here to be obedient to what God has called me to do. Success looks different to those of us who minister in dire settings. It's not about the tangibles, what you can see or measure, even though those exist: the student who graduates instead of dropping out; the young man who rejects gang life, learns a trade, and is ready to start a family; the boy who grew up in the streets surviving to adulthood and having the resources to pursue a fulfilling life. However, it is often about the intangibles: the families whose devotion to Christ helps them to persevere, the joy on the faces of young people experiencing a new thing at camp. Additionally, for me, it's a sense of knowing God's will for my life and being true to it. So yes, I consider myself a success, by God's grace. God led me to this place and God is here. I am happy to be here where God is, serving God's people.

The truth of the matter is that by society's terms, ministry in the inner city among the "least of these" in not a venture that yields a lot of success by worldly standards. The urban ministry practitioner in the trenches is not likely to get rich or become famous. The urban ministry practitioner will not be successful in the sense that the life of every young person they engage will be changed. Young men will continue to be murdered, children will go hungry, families will experience devastating crises, and injustices will abound; however, to stand up for the disempowered in Jesus's name and help the poor, feed the hungry, assist the lame have eternal significance. These acts fall in line with what Jesus had to say about himself in Luke 4, why he had come and what he'd come to do.

And so, this book and the accompanying resources are meant to help the person who carries a burden to work with youth in the inner city. While it is tailored to address the specific needs of African American boys in urban communities, its principles are applicable to all youth, whatever the gender, ethnicity, or socioeconomic status—addressing issues of self-esteem, belonging, empowerment, and one's identity in Christ. For the pastor, youth worker, or volunteer who wants to impact the lives of youth around them on a relational level, this book is a must. It is not about programs or sensational activities, it's about presence and relationship. This is not a program with a definite starting or ending point. This book will direct you on how to follow a lifelong relational process. There are many aids for doing ministry. *Not Forsaken* is a sharing of this minister's stories and experiences and an invitation for you to begin the journey.

The principles and insights I share are meant to be an aid to those who are working out their own call to minister in the city, particularly among Black youth. I hope that these insights and reflections will answer some questions and bring clarity, inspiring and motivating others to trust God and do the work necessary for God to use them to bear fruit in difficult communities. Consider me as an experienced resource. By God's grace Christ's Children Ministries has borne much fruit in our community through the lives of young people who are now carrying out God's work in their own way: as teachers and coaches, accountants, electricians, carpenters, and yes, as ministers.

It is not about duplication. Each ministry will be different. Each person has unique God-imbued gifts and abilities, which when utilized will manifest themselves in birthing unique and various ministries. Our goal together as the Church is to lift up the name of Christ and to build up and edify one another. So my hope is that urban practitioners who read this book may find some kernel of inspiration or find some useful tool that will equip them to use their own gifts to greater effect to the glory of God among the people of God.

CHAPTER ONE

THE COLOR OF GOD

JAMES

A resident of our neighborhood, James, had been a child when we became friends. He was involved with our ministry through various activities, trips, mentoring, and our teen discipleship group. James was not a gangbanger or street thug. His troubles stemmed from dysfunction at home . . . parents who struggled with drug addiction. He was one of the "rank and file" Black male youth in urban communities not actively engaged in negativism or violence, yet he was at-risk due to living in violent, crime-ridden, and poverty-stricken environments. He was a quiet sort, soft-spoken and generally polite, but you could never be sure what he was thinking. When he did feel strongly about something, he would let you know.

James was fifteen when we began to spend a lot of time together in a mentoring relationship. At seventeen he became interested in Black Nationalism, drawn by its militancy and pride in being Black. It gave James an outlet for his own frustration and anger about which he became more and more outspoken. Although he had given his life to Christ in one of our Bible study sessions, he was suspicious about all things Christian. He did not trust what he viewed as a White institution. During this time we met outside of the local church where I worked and, walking down an alley, we had a conversation.

Me: James, do you ever go to church?

James: No.

Me: Would you like to come to church with me on Sunday?

James: No way! That church is for White people.

Me: What? Why do you say that?

James: Because White people go to that church, and besides everyone knows that Jesus is White.

Me: Not everyone, I don't know any such thing.

James: Jesus is White and Christianity is a White man's religion. I'm going to join the Nation of Islam because Black Muslims worship Allah and he is Black.

Me: James, first of all, Jesus was not White. He was born in a part of the world where everyone was of mixed African and Asian heritage. Second of all, Black people go to church here too. And third of all, Christianity is not a White religion because God is not White. Every ethnic group in the world came from God! God is every color!

James: Well, they have a picture of Jesus in that church and he's White. How come every time you see a picture of Jesus he is a White man?

We had reached the part of the alley directly behind my church. Entering the building I asked, "Have you never seen a picture of Jesus and he was not White?" I had rarely seen any myself so it was not a surprise when he said no. I took James into the church library to see a woodcarving of the Last Supper. All the figures in the carving have African features (broad noses, kinky hair, thick lips). He stared at it for a while, then said, "That's supposed to be Jesus? He looks like me!"

Me: The artist is Kenyan. This is what he thought Jesus looked like. Since no artist today has seen Jesus face to face, who can criticize his representation of Christ? Christianity started over in the Middle East where people were mixed African and Asian descent. In fact, the Christian Church in the first few centuries grew mostly in North Africa. Jesus was born a Hebrew in the Middle East. He had African blood in him like all the people in that area of the world. If he lived in America today he'd be considered Black because he had African blood. He lived in the desert, man! He was a lot darker than *all* the pictures you've seen.

James: I've never seen Jesus like that. That's cool.

I then took James to my office to see another portrayal of a Black Jesus. James was silent, clearly rethinking some of his convictions about who Jesus is.

James was not a bad kid, but being poor and living in the inner city his experience with institutional racism made him not trust the world and society, and thus, the institutional Church. His Blackness marked him for several of society's prejudices regardless of his personal conduct or behavior; he had experienced racism at school, in the neighborhood, and in public places. James, like many Black male youth, responded to this injustice with anger and hostility. While not destructive or violent, James drew a lot of his self-image from militant ideas about what it meant to be Black in a society that distrusts and fears Black people. His concept of Christianity and religion in general was colored by this perspective.

Our encounter challenged some of his own presuppositions about being alienated from God and Church because of race and ethnicity. He assumed that the Church and God would be just like the rest of the world he had experienced: fearful, distrustful, and alienating. And truth be told, oftentimes the Church is just that to society's disenfranchised. But through this conversation, James began to see Christ in a different light and from a perspective that affirmed who he was as a young Black man. He began to craft a new, and accurate, self-image of being Christian and Black. Not long afterward, he was pressured by his father to quit school and get a full-time job to help with family expenses. After he dropped out of school he drifted away from our friendship, becoming more involved in street life, drugs, and gangs. When his father died from health complications, I was able to be there for him. Eventually, he got cleaned up and is living a positive life.

When I think of James, it is hard to define success, or evaluate my impact on his life. I believe, as *The Gospel According to Peanuts* explains, "the 'success' of all Christian witnessing finally lies in the hands of God."[1] I knew that I could not "save" James, but I could love him and be his friend. And through this, he has seen that God loves him and embraces him as a Black person, an insight he was unable to gain from institutional Christianity. He is drug-free, working, and has hopes for a better life. Many of his peers are dead, addicted to drugs, or in jail. Based on that day when he gave his life to Christ, in prayer on my living room floor, I know he is a Christian. And although he is not living what some in evangelical Christian circles may consider an overtly Christian lifestyle with regular church attendance and so forth, James has faith and hope in Christ.

THE COLOR OF GOD

What color is God? What color is Christ? Does it matter? Evangelical Christianity often dismisses questions like these with responses of the color blindness of Christianity. However, this issue is extremely relevant for working with and discipling Black male youth in the city. In dismissing or overlooking issues of ethnicity or culture, we ignore the essences of a person's being. All youth go through a period of exploring who they are and what they stand for. It was difficult for James to identify with Christianity or the Church because to him they represented White culture. He was drawn to Nation of Islam because he viewed it as being for Black people. His relationship with me caused him to rethink many of his observations and suppositions about a Black person's spirituality. He struggled with his self-identity in relationship to God and religion. Was he a proud Black man or a Christian? For him Black spirituality was an either/or proposition.

The issue of Jesus's ethnicity is important to urban Black male youth, to be more exact, the issue of personal identification with Christ, culturally, ethnically, and socially. For many youth like James, real and genuine connection with Christ doesn't happen until the issue of identification is addressed. All the church camps, Bible studies, and other activities will have limited effect until a young person with self-image issues can personally identify in some way with Christ.

Historically, society's institutions have systematically devalued Black people, and tragically the institutional Church has done its part to maintain that status quo. So we, the Church, must ask ourselves, Are we presenting the gospel in a way that urban Black male youth may relate to it? Can they find commonality with God, Christianity, or the Christian Church, or is it all alien to their life experience? When asked to draw pictures of God, children in my neighborhood invariably come up with an image of an old White man with a white beard. Our young people need to be able to see themselves in Christ.

Young Black males in the city need to know that God is the author of Blackness. God is the author of every ethnicity and culture in creation. Blackness comes from God! To be authentically Black means being connected to God. The late urban evangelist and prophet Tom Skinner asserts in *How Black Is the Gospel?* that Black people must embrace our Blackness in following Christ:

> Now that Jesus Christ lives in me I know who I am—I'm a son of God. This doesn't mean I have negated my blackness. The gospel of Jesus Christ is black in the sense that it does not ask a Black man to give up his blackness to be a Christian. . . . I am a black man in whom God is living. Black is beautiful . . . since Jesus Christ is living through it, and one of the things I have discovered is that Jesus looks great in black.[2]

This book had a tremendous influence on me as a young minister in an urban community. You see, all my life I'd been confronted with people's different ideas about what it means to be Black. I was often disparaged as a youth for not being "Black" enough: for not having the right hair, or wearing the right clothes, for speaking with clear diction, for liking to learn and read books. I experienced racism from White people and dissatisfaction from Black people. Nobody would let me just be who I was. In the hood I wasn't bad enough. I didn't smoke, drink, or cuss. I didn't engage in self-destructive behavior like crime, gangs, or drugs.

In the Church, I was encouraged to stay with my own people or be a token within a White congregation. Everybody was telling me who I was and what it meant to be Black. When I read Skinner's book, it was like the scales had fallen off of my eyes and my life made sense. Why should I listen to anyone's ideas about being Black? Instead, I could go to the source—God! And so I found freedom to be who I was, a Black Man, without having to submit to anyone else's expectations. This is what young people need, permission to be who they are in Christ. Young males in the city are searching for a way to relate to God and they miss out on this essential connection because no one teaches it or shares it with them—supposedly because color and race don't matter.

Race matters. There is no authentic Blackness apart from God. This concept is critically important to building the self-esteem of urban Black young men. We must take pains to teach young men in the city who are suffering from cultural oppression who they are in Christ. These young men need to know where they come from.

If you are a young Black male and have repeatedly been exposed to negative messages about Black manhood either through your environment, the media, or even peers and family, being affirmed for who you are ethnically is a critical step in becoming open to the gospel. What does it mean, from the perspective of the young urban Black male, to be created in God's image? If they were convinced that their Blackness comes from God, perhaps the overwhelming negative trends plaguing young Black men in education, crime, imprisonment, and employment would change for the better; perhaps, fewer would fall prey to negative and immoral models of Black manhood or succumb to the stresses and pressures of living daily under the scrutiny of a society in which they feel like second-class citizens.

Is it possible for young urban Black males to genuinely identify with Christianity? When I first moved into my neighborhood I couldn't get many of the young people I worked with to come to my church because they considered it a White church and Christianity a White religion. James is just one example. I wondered if they would react that way if they knew that Christianity has its roots in North Africa. The monastic movement that followed the period of martyrdom in the history of Christianity was a tremendously significant time in the growth of Church theology and policy. The center of this movement was in North Africa. Augustine, one of the early church fathers and author of the theological tome *City of God*, was an African. Christianity is not a White religion any more than it is a Black religion. Black youth need to be educated on these facts.

In the first century, the city of Antioch was a major center of commerce and trade in the world, and the church there was the center for leadership in the fledgling Christian movement. In fact, it was at Antioch that the word *Christian* was first coined in reference to followers of Christ, meaning "little Christs" (Acts 11:26). A roster of the first church board appears in Acts 13:1. In this chapter, the church elders send Barnabas and Paul on a missionary journey with the laying on of hands and prayer. Two of the five men listed are identified as follows: Simeon, called Niger (which can be translated "the Black man"), and Lucius of Cyrene. Cyrene was a city in North Africa. A man identified as being Black and one who was African helped lead and develop the early Church.

Once apprised of these facts, Black youth could hardly consider Christianity a White religion. It is a tragedy for Black youth to lose interest in Christianity because they fail to identify with it. The scholarship of Cain Hope Felder points out the heritage of Jesus, along with everyone else in that part of the world, as being mixed African and Asian. "Scholars today generally recognize that the biblical Hebrews [Jews] most likely emerged as an amalgamation of races, rather than from any pure racial stock. When they departed from Egypt they may well have been Afro-Asiatics."[3]

By the standards of American society, Jesus himself was a Black man. According to the "one drop" rule of the Jim Crow South, if a person had one drop of African blood he or she would be considered Black. Jesus had more than a drop. In my neighborhood, he would be referred to as a light-skinned brother. Ethnically, Jesus was Jewish, but his appearance and heritage are natural points of identification with the gospel for young Black males. These essential and relevant truths should be shared with all Christians seeking the truth, especially with Black youth looking for a point of connection with Christianity. They are not shared, partly because of our ignorance, and also because of fear of a Black God.

FEAR OF A BLACK GOD

Christ is relevant for the issues facing youth today because he can uniquely relate to their experience. Black boys growing up in inner-city communities face a legacy of poverty, racism, and violence. As a boy, Jesus faced extermination when King Herod ordered all Hebrew boys slaughtered in an attempt to kill the prophesied future king. Jesus experienced racism as a Jew in the Roman Empire, living in Roman-occupied Israel. (The Romans were European, imposing a Greco-Roman culture throughout the Roman Empire.) He spent most of his life with the poor, oppressed, and ostracized of his society. (His parents were poor as indicated by their offering of birds when he was circumcised [Luke 2:24; Leviticus 12:6-8].) We've already seen that in America, because of his lineage, Jesus would be considered a Black man, having a dual African/Asian heritage. Jesus knew what it was like to be discriminated against and to be feared and hated because of his ethnic background. He knew what it was like to live an endangered life, and he knew what it was like to be Black. Jesus knew what it was like to grow up male, and he knew what it was like to be poor. Jesus Christ can speak to the issues facing young Black males in America.

To get a sense of the unique emotional stresses associated with being Black and male in urban America, consider the following story about three youth. Active in our ministry for several years, they went on a mission trip to Monterrey, Mexico. These guys were wonderful, interesting people, full of life and humor, and possessing street smarts—that is—a certain kind of wisdom cultivated not through conventional means such as school and books but through experiencing the often difficult circumstances in which they had grown. They were young Christians, learning who they are in Christ. They were handsome in physical appearance as well as in spirit, with great potential as leaders for our society. Yet they were all struggling in various ways with institutional racism, community dysfunction, and low self-image.

The miracle of this trip was that for the duration, they were in the company of people who saw and affirmed their positive qualities. To say that everyone liked them would be an understatement. From the beginning of the trip these young men emerged as leaders and set an example and tone for the trip, which was emulated by other youth. Adults valued and appreciated them, their peers respected them, younger children looked up to them. Never before had they experienced this kind of affirmation. Each afternoon when we returned to the home where we were staying, a crowd of neighborhood children would surround and follow the boys, chattering excitedly in Spanish, and clamoring for their attention. Everyone was impressed by their personality, charisma, and poise. At home they were always under the cloud of suspicion and racism—but in Mexico they were esteemed for their obvious gifts and talents.

Each experienced God's presence in tremendous ways during the week; they grew spiritually and were able to see themselves in a new light.

In the hood, a young Black male's self-concept is under constant attack from negative influences. I feel it every day and I'm a grown man. The devastating impact of institutional racism in our culture on young people is hard to express. Each day we must wage a war for the preservation of self-image in the face of suspicious police officers, distrusting store clerks, indifferent teachers, and peers without hope. It's like trying to keep your head above water in the ocean; you can't stop treading water or you'll be overwhelmed by the next wave. Facing issues of poverty and dysfunction at home feels like an anchor, dragging you down. There are few places where these young men receive regular affirmation for the quality people that they are. But in Mexico, it was different. Everyone could see who they really were, without the baggage of a prejudiced and fearful society. These young men know who they are; it was nice to spend time in a place where others knew it too.

What would it be like if Jesus showed up now, in this time, a poor African American male? An excellent video, *The Second Coming*,[4] poses this exact question and yields some incredible insights. The video's premise is that when African American Jesus returns for the Second Coming, he faces a scenario that is historically common for Black males in America. He is falsely accused, arrested, imprisoned, and convicted on a charge of rape of a little White girl. If he had come in the late 1800s to mid-1900s, he surely would've been lynched. Black men were being dragged out of their homes and lynched by White mobs for accusations just such as this. In this period of American history at least five thousand people were killed in horrible ways in the name of White supremacy.

In the video, the main body of evidence against Jesus is that he fits the description of the perpetrator. Just before he is to be executed, he vanishes and returns to God's side, taking many believers with him, as described in Paul's account of Jesus's return (1 Thessalonians 4:15-17). As Jesus described in Matthew 24:40-41, some folks you think would get left behind go to heaven with Jesus; and some that you think would go with Jesus get left behind. In describing a scenario of what would happen if Jesus came back today, the film challenges observers' preconceptions about Christ and about what it means to be a follower of Christ.

> ## God is not "color-blind." God made the rich and beautiful variety of cultures, ethnicities, and skin hues that make up humanity.

The affirmation that Jesus is Black, or, at least, not White, is a contentious topic in many evangelical and ecclesiological settings. People of color often are put in a position of having to mount a coup in order for the institutional Church to consider a non-White/European perspective on the gospel. Over the ages Jesus has been portrayed in many ways by cultures of differing ethnicities. In mainstream Catholic and Protestant churches, Jesus has been portrayed as being White for centuries. Yet, we are told that color doesn't matter; that God— thereby the Church—is color-blind. But we who are people of color know that color matters in this world. God is not "color-blind." God made the rich and beautiful variety of cultures, ethnicities, and skin hues that make up humanity. It is the height of hubris to subvert God's design in any way. God is the author of difference and diversity.

The Church is to be in the world but not of it, but we struggle with this. As Dr. King often remarked, Sunday morning at eleven o'clock continues to be the most segregated hour in America. We do our young people a disservice if we do not address issues like this head-on. In doing so, we are serving the Church and society as well as our young people. At the same time, if we only emphasize the ethnicity of Jesus, then we miss the whole point of Christ. The point of this book is that Black male youth in the city should be able to see themselves in Christ.

Mainstream society is afraid of a Black God. God, of course, is Spirit (John 4:24), and as such we cannot limit God with human descriptions of ethnicity, gender, or geographical or political boundaries. God, however, is not offended when an Asian person envisions God or Christ with Asian features, or a Latino person envisions God with Latin characteristics, the same with African, European, and so on. God is the author of all ethnicities and cultures. God's goodness and glory are manifested in each one. But there exists this fear of a

Black God because of the implications of how Black people have been treated in America.

Imagine if a group of people who had been oppressed for centuries in society suddenly became the power brokers of that society. The former power brokers would live in fear of what the new regime would do. This is fear of a Black God, a fear derived from centuries of the debasement of Black people in this country. American society struggles with its *sin of the enslavement and subjugation of a people and is distrustful of all things Black*. The Church also, as an institution, shares in this guilt and this is what I refer to as *fear of a Black God*.

Storekeepers' eyes follow Black youth when they enter their stores for fear they will steal something. Crowds of Black youth are viewed with suspicion and fear, and subsequently discouraged from meeting in public places. Police harass and follow groups of Black youth innocently walking down the street. These occurrences are commonplace in inner-city neighborhoods. Black drivers have been stopped so frequently compared to the general population that the term "driving while Black" was coined. School suspension rates, disparity in achievement, disproportionate appearances in court, and a terribly skewed prison population: these and other systemic representations of racism point to a societal fear of Black people, and not just Black people but all who are oppressed and unfairly treated in our midst. As the late James Cone suggests in his book *A Black Theology of Liberation*, a Black God is a God of the oppressed. American society should be afraid to incur God's wrath. The Book of Amos (5:11) tells us how God's judgment came upon Israel for their mistreatment of the poor among them and their lack of repentance.

When Nelson Mandela was released after years of imprisonment in South Africa and the system of apartheid finally began to dissolve, the existing government and mainstream culture were full of trepidation over what might happen. Afrikaaners were afraid that South African Blacks would retaliate if they came to power following years of abuse and suffering under the system of apartheid (fear of an African God). The Truth and Reconciliation Commission was formed to settle injustices and foment peace and reconciliation. The same fear was operating in the United States during the Reconstruction period following the Civil War. As a nation, America needed its own Truth and Reconciliation Commission. Instead, when Blacks gained political power in the South

through the right to vote and gained representation in government, White politicians, through backroom deals, invented laws and practices that subverted
and usurped that power.

Mainstream society doesn't want to be reminded that Jesus was Black,
poor, and oppressed because it hits too close to home. Society would have to
consider the implications of how it treats people in our midst, the people it
encounters each day as individuals who suffer and are oppressed or mistreated.
In the parable of the sheep and the goats in Matthew 25:31-46, we see that
the reward of the goats who mistreated or ignored Jesus in the guise of the
thirsty, the hungry, the stranger, and the prisoner as eternal separation from
God. Mainstream society is afraid of a Black God because that would mean
acknowledging the many societal sins of which it is unrepentant and perhaps
being judged for them. To follow Christ, the Church must see the poor,
oppressed, Jewish Christ of the Bible in the homeless person on the corner
asking for work or food, in the troubled young people in our communities, in
families living in poverty, in the newly arrived immigrant, and in the unjustly
accused or imprisoned.

IDENTIFICATION WITH CHRIST

In actuality, the level of identification the young Black male may experience
with Christ extends beyond the physicality of ethnicity to social, emotional,
and spiritual depths. Economic disparity is another point of identification.
Current statistical data indicates that 33 percent of Black children are born in
poverty. Relative to the culture of the time, Jesus was born into a poor family.
In Luke 2:22-24, the sacrifice offered by Mary and Joseph for their firstborn
male child was a pair of doves or two young pigeons. Leviticus 12:8 stipulates
that this offering is acceptable if a family cannot afford the usual sacrifice of a
young lamb. In today's society, Jesus's parents would be considered as being
among the "working poor."

Another point of identification Black male youth may have with Christ
is housing instability. When Jesus was grown and ministering with his disciples, he said, "Foxes have dens and birds have nests, but the Son of Man has
no place to lay his head" (Luke 9:58 NIV), which indicates housing instability

and possible homelessness. In our ministry, families move quite frequently as a result of financial distress, eviction, and family crises. It is not unusual for youth in our ministry to change living locations two or three times a year. It is a challenge to follow our kids because they do not leave forwarding addresses or give notice when they move. One has to be in relationship in order to pick up the clues of transition. African American families made up more than half (51.7 percent) of families with children in shelters in 2016.[5]

Christ led an endangered life, another dynamic through which urban Black male youth may relate. Jesus was threatened by zealous Jews. Religious leaders tried to kill him because of his claims of being the Messiah (Luke 4:28-30), because of his challenge to their authority (19:45-48), and because they were afraid of his power and influence (Mark 3:5-6). After Jesus was born, his family had to flee to Egypt as refugees due to King Herod's efforts to have him murdered (Matthew 2:13-18) by executing all the young boys in the area of his birth. Jamar Clark and Philando Castile (both in the Minneapolis/St. Paul area) and a host of young Black men across the country similarly had their lives stolen from them by overzealous police. Black young men are endangered in the city, having disproportionate rates of homicide, incarceration, and health risks.

Jesus experienced racial discrimination as a Jew in Roman-occupied Judea. Inner-city Black male youth can certainly identify with this. Jesus was harassed by Roman soldiers who felt like it was the duty of citizens of an occupied territory to give up the very shirt off their backs to serve a representative of Rome (Matthew 5:38-42). We can infer that many Jews of Jesus's time felt emasculated by a lack of power. Their country had been occupied by Rome and they did not have the freedom to govern themselves and freely follow their religious customs. This agitation culminated in the Jewish/Roman War of 66 CE.

As a young man, Jesus likely shared those feelings and experienced the marginalization of Jewish communities. The experience of Christ in terms of racial and ethnic discrimination elicits a strong comparison to the plight of the Black male in urban communities in American cities. Young Black men are subjected to racial profiling by police through stop and search laws and "driving while Black" practices. Due to institutional racism Black men are more likely to be arrested, convicted, and incarcerated than their White counterparts for the same behaviors. And Black boys continue to struggle in educational systems where their numbers are grossly overrepresented for behavior, suspension, and low achievement.

A starkly defining point of identification is how Jesus's life ended. Jesus was unjustly accused, wrongfully convicted of, and executed for crimes he did not commit. The Jewish religious leaders convicted him of blasphemy, a crime punishable by death under Jewish law (Leviticus 24:15-16), for not disaffirming that he was the Son of God (Luke 22:66-71). However, the Jewish court, the Sanhedrin, did not have the power to carry out capital punishments. This is why he was turned over to the Roman government. Even though Jesus also would not disaffirm that he was king of the Jews, Pilate could find no basis for a conviction. Nevertheless, the Romans executed him for fear of rebellion, due to his kingdom teachings, actions of acting out the role of an anointed king (Mark 11:7-11), and popularity with the people (Luke 23:1-5). An unjust court system sentenced him to death.

I advise the boys I work with that the best protection from an unjust court system is to not let yourself be in a circumstance that may end up with you in front of a judge; the reality is that it is imperative for them to avoid this situation. And when this happens, they cannot expect fair and impartial treatment. The Equal Justice Initiative describes the situation:

> Black children are more than twice as likely as white kids to be arrested, but the data shows this disparity is not because Black kids are committing more crimes, *Mother Jones* reports. Black youth are burdened by a presumption of guilt and dangerousness—a legacy of our history of racial injustice that marks youth of color for disparately frequent stops, searches, and violence and leads to higher rates of childhood suspension, expulsion, and arrest at school; disproportionate contact with the juvenile justice system; harsher charging decisions and disadvantaged plea negotiations; a greater likelihood of being denied bail and diversion; an increased risk of wrongful convictions and unfair sentences; and higher rates of probation and parole revocation.[6]

Jesus died on the cross, having been crucified; crucifixion being the instrument of state-sanctioned execution of the time. Jesus's cry, "My God, my God, why have you forsaken me?" indicated that in the isolation of his suffering, he felt utterly alone and completely abandoned. Passages in the Book of Isaiah have been interpreted as relating to God's servant (Isaiah 52:13-15), a Messianic figure, who would be given over to his enemies, persecuted, and abused. Most Christians believe that these prophecies were fulfilled in Jesus, the Christ, which means "Anointed One" in Greek, the equivalent of what Messiah means in Hebrew. "He was despised and avoided by others; / a man who suffered, who knew sickness well. / Like someone from whom people hid their faces, / he was despised, and we didn't think about him" (Isaiah 53:3). "He was oppressed and tormented" (53:7a). "Due to an unjust ruling he was taken away, / and his fate—who will think about it?" (53:8a).

Black men are disproportionately represented in our penal system, both in regular prison populations and on death row. They are six times as likely to be incarcerated as White men. Black men make up roughly one third of our prison population[7] while the entire Black population is only 13 percent of our nation's population. Of inmates on death row, Black people make up 42 percent.[8] Ironically, the passion of Christ may be the greatest point by which young men may relate to Christ. Who can imagine their future?

Suffering and oppression are an everyday reality for the segment of American society that is Black, poor, and male. Young Black men are close to Christ by virtue of their suffering. They may identify with Christ but more importantly, God identifies with them. From Herod's genocidal edict against Hebrew males at Jesus's birth to an effective genocide of the African American male in urban communities, God is on the side of those who are suffering and oppressed. Cone illustrates the Blackness of God:

> The blackness of God, and everything implied by it in a racist society, is the heart of the black theology doctrine of God. There is no place in black theology for a colorless God in a society where human beings suffer precisely because of their color. . . . Either God is identified with the oppressed to the point that their experience becomes God's experience, or God is a God of racism.[9]

God is Black because God identifies with the poor and oppressed.

CONCLUSION

The question, *What color is God?* is significant because it is a query about one's origins and a quest for belonging. To affirm that God is Black fills the need for spiritual identity that is crucial for one's self-esteem. Rather than excluding other cultures, it is a statement of inclusion of all cultures. This assertion is critical in order to overcome the unique and often overwhelming societal stress Black kids face. They can relate to God and Christ because God understands them and their life experience. To state that God is Black is to say God is a God of the suffering. By virtue of the sacrament of suffering, the eternal blessings of Christ are experienced by those who suffer in a way those who have not known deep suffering will never experience in this world. Suffering brings one to a state of reliance and dependence on God and that produces a depth of relationship, faith, and knowledge of God that cannot be experienced otherwise (2 Corinthians 1:8-10).

People who take on the responsibility of discipling Black male youth must take into account their particular culture of suffering and oppression. The Blackness of God is not so much about the ethnicity of God or Christ, but about the nature of God to stand with the poor and oppressed, in spirit and in daily life. Connection to God is about the capacity of individuals who have seen or experienced little or no self-worth or affirmation to see themselves not only as persons about whom God cares, but also as persons whom God created and cherishes. The core aim of discipling young people is for them to know who they are in Christ. Not as African Americans, not as Black men or youth, but first as children of God. It is incumbent upon the Church to use all the tools God has given the Church to break through the formidable barriers of hatred, injustice, and racism to allow individuals to embrace the truth of God's love. And because God loves Black boys, there is no obstacle they cannot surmount in order to have the life for which God created them.

CHAPTER TWO
BECOMING A MAN

TERRY

Terry was part of a group of teenaged boys with whom I had been working for about five years. On this day, the topic of discussion was what they were going to do when they grew up. They were all in the ninth and tenth grades at school, and while they had grown out of the "I'm gonna be an NFL football player" stage, most of their answers were vague. We talked about college, trade school, and other possibilities. The fifteen-year-old Terry replied, "I don't know, but I better have a job because my dad is going to kick me out when I'm eighteen." On the surface this may sound harsh, but Terry's answer was the most real of the group. Over the next few years, Terry's overriding concern was being able to take care of himself or contribute to the household when he became an adult. The others did not have dads at home; they also didn't have the same sense of urgency about becoming adults or being able to take care of themselves.

After his sophomore year in high school, Terry dropped out of school. When I challenged him about it, he said he had to work. He wasn't doing well in school so his dad said he had to quit and get a job. I knew Terry's dad because

I had visited in their home often. This man was determined that his boys would not succumb to the street life that claimed him at a young age. However, he and I disagreed over how best to meet that goal. A year later, Terry was moving from job to job, not finding anything regular, and lacking the skills and education for a good prospect. While he attended church and my discipleship group regularly, it seemed like his life was heading nowhere, and he would soon be eighteen. Now, Terry and his girlfriend were expecting a baby. He escaped his father's ultimatum of eviction by moving in with her. But he still had to work and temporary labor would not take care of his family. He got a part-time job and I helped him begin a GED course.

During this whole period, rather than being depressed and/or angry with his dad, Terry was energized and motivated. He just kept trying to get things right, no matter how difficult the path. He kept trying. He avoided the streets, drugs, and gangs. This was no easy task because he was part of a gang family. His peers, including his little brother, kept telling him to forget that girl and her baby, join their gang, and live it up. But Terry wanted to grow up. He wanted to be a man. His parents, who had cleaned up their lives quite a bit by this time, saw how hard he was trying. His mother helped him get a job where she worked. He completed his GED. He became a devoted father. In the eyes of his family and peers, Terry became a man. Terry is a success story in the neighborhood. He's alive, unsullied by drugs, and working a job making decent wages.

I watched Terry grow up; I was with him in good times and bad. We played basketball, went on trips, did church and Bible study. I stood by him when he got in gang fights, dropped out of high school, and became a teenaged father. As his pastor and confidant, I helped him to stay connected to God through all the changes in his life. I believe that this impact was possible through cultivating a strong relationship with him and his family.

As the eldest of five siblings, Terry was conscious of the responsibility that traditionally came with that position in families. Even though his parents struggled with drug addiction, they were able to maintain one of the more stable family-oriented cultures in the community. Terry's father was present in the home. Despite his own problems of participating in gang culture and chemical addictions, he wanted Terry to avoid them and was successful in communicating to Terry a strong sense of what it meant to be a man.

With his father's admonishments, despite being surrounded by drugs and gang life, Terry never seriously fell into any of it. His younger brother was imprisoned for being involved in a gang-related shooting. Peers and extended family became prey to any one of a number of pitfalls facing them. However, Terry had a strong sense of what was right, what he needed to do to survive the hood, and this sense of rightness was directly related to what he thought would please his dad.

Terry's image of manhood could be summed up simply: a man must be able to take care of his responsibilities, primarily his family. Even though he dropped out of school, got a girl pregnant when he was seventeen, and flirted closely with gang life at a certain point, Terry realized that these things would not put him on the path to becoming a man. He got himself together. In addition to completing his GED, he got a good job and stayed with it for many years. He became closely involved with his baby's upbringing. Although a sporadic churchgoer, Terry has been able to stay focused on becoming the person he wanted to be by a relationship with God. Today, I look at Terry and I see him on a path to a meaningful life. He is a good role model for other young men in the community.

THE MANTLE OF MANHOOD

In the course of our relationship, starting when Terry was about twelve years old, he would tell me how much he respected his dad and share things that his dad taught him. He seemed to be asking himself, "How do I become a man?" His concern that by age eighteen he needed a good job or his dad would kick him out of the house was a clear message of the expectation of providing for one's self as a stage of maturity. Terry's dad answered the question of manhood for him in many ways, and it proved to be a guide for him in a critical period of his life.

My parents also taught me and my brothers that an adult male was expected to be able to provide for himself. Our father's message was similar to Terry's dad, that if we weren't in college at eighteen, we'd have to get a job or join the army. Otherwise, he'd kick us out of the house because he wasn't going to support us. Our parents provided for us in childhood: a roof over our heads, food on the table, and clothes on our backs. They provided money to go on camping trips, jobs for spare change, and so on.

As a youth I hated to ask my dad for money and I knew I was a man when I didn't have to ask him for any. My dad is "old school." He didn't get anything in his life for free and was offended when one of us kids asked for money without having done something to earn it. He would look at you like you were crazy for expecting him to just hand over some money without your having earned it. Then he would list all the chores—apart from our regular chores around the house and yard—that needed to be done. Eventually, we kids got the point. One day when I was away at college, I called home to check in with the folks and my dad asked if I needed anything. I thought about it. I was managing my tuition with loans and financial aid. I had a job so I could have pocket money for expenses, dates, and supplies. There were a number of things I wanted, but nothing I needed from him. So I said "Naw, Dad. I'm all right." That's when I knew I was a man.

Young Black boys are asking themselves:

- How do I become a man?
- What kind of man do I want to be?
- What does a real man look like?
- Who can tell me?

Too many of them have no positive male role model (father, uncle, brother, pastor, teacher) to provide some guidance. What if the father is not providing a positive image of manhood? Who picks up the slack? How do they find out what it means to be a man? According to the latest census information in 2010, 65.3 percent of Black children are born to single parent families. In my neighborhood, 60 percent of families in poverty are headed by single moms. If dad is not home, or if dad is home but is not being a good father, who bestows the mantle of manhood on Black boys? Many single mothers are doing tremendous jobs raising their sons to be strong and responsible men. However, some in this situation are struggling just to provide their children's basic physical needs, and tragically boys are left to themselves to figure out the whole manhood thing.

Where do young men, who want a different outcome and an alternative lifestyle to the macho, gangbanging, and violent images of manhood confronting them daily, turn? They are either oblivious to alternatives or consider them unattainable. They struggle for the recognition and respect that adulthood brings. Whether it is the street, the home, or the peer group, the answers to the questions raised reveal the quality of manhood to which a young person aspires. Absentee fathers, male relatives, friends, or neighbors, knowingly or unknowingly set the standard for manhood and bestow the mantle of adulthood. In my years of doing ministry among these kids, a checklist of what it means to be a man has emerged:

- You have to be hard. Don't show any weakness by exhibiting "soft" emotions.
- Harbor no disrespect. Don't let anyone challenge your manhood or belittle you in any way.
- Gain respect by cultivating a reputation for harsh behavior so that others fear you.
- You gotta be "down," ready and willing to do what it takes to get what you need, including acts of violence.

For many young men growing up in the city, often it is your "boys" (friends) who let you know whether you are a man or not. For better or worse, their peers are the most consistent relationships these young men may have.

In a perfect world, the mantle of manhood should come from the family. My parents let me know when I would be a man by showing me how a man looks and behaves, and together instilling those values within me. For them, it was about self-sufficiency and personal satisfaction. My mom used to tell me when I was young, "Chris, it doesn't matter what you do in life as long as you can take care of yourself and you are content." My understanding was this: 1) Can I take care of myself and others I care for? 2) Am I satisfied/content with my life?

My parents were not rich. To some, they may have seemed poor. But my siblings and I never wanted for anything we needed in life. Although there were plenty of times of scarcity, we never suffered the lack of some need so that my parents could enjoy some fleeting pleasure or possession. Their example was not lost on me. My dad got up early every day and went to work. He came home at night and we ate dinner as a family. My mom worked as well and took care of the family. My siblings and I had chores and responsibilities to help take care of the house. We had structure, discipline, and consequences for inappropriate behavior. Although there were many things we wanted as kids and could not afford, we never went hungry, homeless, or were unprepared for school. These basic experiences shaped my understanding of manhood (indeed adulthood) and responsibility.

Many young Black males in urban neighborhoods receive mixed messages about maturity, if any at all. Negative behavior portrayed by adults in the family circle indelibly imprint young people with erroneous images of what it means to be adult. Many poor, Black families are reduced to simply surviving from day to day. Communities are full of heroic single mothers who valiantly and often successfully raise their boys to become men. The struggle of single moms to achieve their goals are exacerbated by either the absence of positive male role models or the presence of negative ones. The careful nurture of emerging manhood becomes a task that is abdicated to the streets or peer group, where men may model inebriation, criminal activity, gang involvement, or sexual promiscuity as characteristics of manhood. When adults in the home are unable or unwilling to parent, they leave this responsibility to whoever will take it up, for good or bad. In addition to the normal stresses of growing up, a young boy with an absent father may have questions:

- Where is my dad? Is he alive, dead, or in jail?
- Does he care about me? Is he thinking of me?
- Does he have another family? Does he hate me?
- Am I the reason he left?

This is the reality of fatherhood experienced by too many Black boys in communities like mine.

RITES OF PASSAGE

Rites of passage play an important role in human development. They are social and/or religious rituals or observances that signal the movement of one stage of life to another. The Latin *quinceañera* for when a girl turns fifteen, Sweet Sixteen parties, cotillions or debutante parties, birthday and retirement celebrations are examples. In the Jewish community, there is the *bar/bat mitzvah*,

22

at the end of which the celebrant specifically says, "Today I am a man!" or "Today I am a woman!" In the Church, there is first communion, baptism, and confirmation. We have political rites such as becoming old enough to buy alcohol legally, to vote, or to register for the draft. Even marriage is a rite of passage. Rites of passage acknowledge a milestone of growth in a young person's life on the way to adulthood. However, they are usually not just for the individual or family alone; they are communal. Rites of passage for youth include the involvement and affirmation of the community in the life of the young person in question, invoking the African proverb, "It takes a village to raise a child." They are a strong part of the cultural heritage of African Americans going all the way back to tribal life in African villages.

I heard this story about rites of passage to manhood concerning the Maasai tribe on a trip I made to East Africa. The Maasai people are a semi-nomadic ethnic group that inhabits northern, central, and southern Kenya and northern Tanzania.

> One misty morning, five Maasai boys rise, leave their village, and go out into the savanna together. (A savanna is a woodland-grassland ecosystem.) They are of the age to participate in rites of manhood, one of which is to kill a lion. If they accomplish this, they will have completed one of the tasks that will enable them to return to their village as men.
>
> Each boy (aged fifteen to twenty-five) has a weapon: a rope, a spear, a knife, a net, and a club. After a while, they come across the tracks of a male lion. Following the tracks, they find him at midafternoon, dozing under a tree. They make plans. If they can tie the rope to the tree and drop a noose over the lion's head, it'll be trapped and they can kill it with their weapons. There's just one problem; someone must distract the lion. The boy with the club sneaks slowly up to the lion while the boy with the rope ties it around the tree. It will be his job to also drop the noose over the lion's head. When the boy with the club smacks the lion on his snout, the lion wakes up with an angry roar. The boy with the rope manages to drop a noose over its head but he does not run away quickly enough and the lion takes a quick swipe at him with its huge paw, killing him instantly.

But the lion is caught. The boy with the spear runs in from one side while the boy with the knife runs in from the other, making jabs and swipes at the lion. The lion is roaring fearfully in anger and the boys are terrified, but determined. The boy with the net manages to get up in the tree and drops the net over the lion from above, trapping it and restricting it from using its sharp claws. The boy with the spear dashes in and impales the lion with a deep thrust, but gets swatted by the lion and thrown several feet, unconscious. The boys with the knife and club run in on the wounded lion and poke and prod and beat on it. The boy in the tree jumps on to the lion's back and grabs the spear in its side, driving it deeper while the lion leaps around trying to shake him off. Holding on for dear life, he manages to drive the spear and pierce the huge beast's heart. The lion screams one final roar of rage and shuddering, falls to the ground—dead.

The boys wake up their unconscious companion and make a stretcher to bear their dead comrade back to the village. They collect trophies from the lion's dead body, including its mane, claws, and tail. Then they return to the village, one step closer to being men.

In many African countries, the days of lion hunting are gone, having been abolished for environmental concerns. And yet there are other rites that Maasai young boys continue to experience as they mature physically to manhood, to gain the rights and privileges of manhood in that culture. Without them, a young man cannot marry, father children, own cattle, or become an elder. The boys mature and grow together in groups or cohorts, going through the different stages of development together. Their transition from boys to men culminates in circumcision, which is borne without anesthesia. After their period of healing, they have completed the necessary rites and rituals to be considered fully grown men among the Maasai people.

In American society, there are many rites of passage for boys and girls on the way to maturity: getting a driver's license, first job, school promotions and graduations. These events were very significant to me growing up. Black boys growing up in low-income neighborhoods, however, typically live out a very different existence. Positive rites of passage such as those that I mentioned have become rare and insignificant; they are not recognized or affirmed, while negative rites have come to be anticipated and regarded as steps to maturity. Common rites of passage for Black males in impoverished communities may include becoming sexually active, fathering a child, going to jail, using drugs, committing a crime, or joining a gang.

When boys in our ministry reach the age of sixteen, I become excited for them. I ask if they will take the driver's education course at school or if they will try to get a job that summer. I remember when I was that age and how important and grown up I felt when I was old enough to do those things. But they do not share my excitement. These opportunities, these rites hold no real significance for them. Oftentimes, they are simply not accessible. They're nonchalant about learning to drive or getting their driver's license. These days, driver's education classes are not available as part of the public-school curriculum, and private courses are expensive. I practically have to drag kids to the Department of Motor Vehicles in order to take their driver's test. Who cares if you have a license when nobody you know owns a car, and the prospects of your owning a car seem about as likely as winning the lottery? And then there are the realities of car ownership, payments, and insurance.

As a teenager, I was so excited to get my first job of delivering newspapers. I had to get up at five o'clock every morning, but I was happy to get that check once a month. Apart from the lure of getting paid, the feeling of independence and self-sufficiency was intoxicating, like I was taking my first step toward manhood. But jobs in urban neighborhoods are scarce for youth and for adults. Suitable jobs that offer skill development and training, building experience for the future, are nonexistent in many urban communities. As an October 2018 article by Paul Davidson in *USA Today* reports,

> Black teen joblessness [19.3 percent] remains well above the broader 12.8 percent teenage unemployment rate. Blacks still face discrimination and often lack a network of contacts who can provide job referrals. . . . They also may live in lower-income neighborhoods that don't have good access to transportation to job sites.[1]

Having a job does not seem like such a thrill or necessity when hardly any of your peers or any men you know has one. They find other ways to independence and self-sufficiency. Alternative rites such as shoplifting, drug-dealing, or robbing people on the streets have become acceptable. They live in a different reality.

Each spring, I attend the eighth-grade graduation of some of our ministry participants. It's a big deal. Their parents come, the kids are dressed up, mothers are crying, gifts are given. For me, the level of celebration is like one would expect at a high school graduation. But when I interact with families whose eighth-grade kids attend private or suburban school, I ask, "How was graduation?" They reply, "What graduation?" They are not having these kinds of celebrations. Their expectation is that students will advance to high school, complete their education in four years, and then there will be cause for celebration.

In urban neighborhoods, many students finishing the eighth grade will not go on to complete their education by graduating from high school. A 2019 article in the Minneapolis *Star Tribune* stated that more than 67 percent of Black students who enrolled in school as ninth-graders graduated in four years. While this is an improvement over past years, it still marks an appalling gap between Black students and White students, whose graduation rate is at 88 percent.[2] Another rite of passage bites the dust!

At first I thought eighth-grade graduations were nice, but upon realizing what they truly mean, they depress me—the rationale being, "This may be the only graduation you experience in life." We are saddling our youth with low expectations. We don't expect them to do much in life, so we settle. It seems as if neither the school system nor parents encourage them or expect them to work hard, overcome obstacles, and achieve according to a societal norm. Underachieving students are enabled by the low expectations of adults.

Life in the hood carries its own unique milestones that constitute rites of passage for young Black men and teenaged boys. These experiences confer a dysfunctional brand of credibility and respect among their peers.

- Black teenaged boys will experience some form of involvement with the penal system. One in three Black males will spend time in jail,[3] and a larger portion have some negative contact with police. Negative contact with the criminal justice system includes being stopped by the police, to having to go to court, to spending time in juvenile detention. The occurrence of these events, even when not initiated by the teen, is a part of growing up Black and male, not only in the inner city but wherever White privilege is found.

- Being sexually active is a rite of passage. Some boys are having sex with girls before they even reach the age where they really like girls. But once it happens, you're in the club. It's not even cool to brag about it; the people who need to know, know, and they see you in a whole different light. It is not unusual in urban communities when teenage boys father children. Although the birth rate among teenaged Black girls has improved drastically over the last two decades, it is still disproportionately higher than that of White girls. Being sexually active and possibly fathering a child is an accepted part of growing up Black and male in the inner city.

- Doing or selling drugs is a common rite. Smoking marijuana (weed, bud, chronic, blunts, joints)—it's all good in the hood. It provides a temporary escape from reality, taking away your pain and anger (for a time), and making you feel good. Some young people start smoking marijuana and their lives become consumed by it. I've seen numerous young males' lives totally derailed by their addiction to smoking. All they want to do is sit around and get high. Employment, relationships, personal dreams, and goals fall by the wayside in the pursuit of getting high. Smoking marijuana saps a person's ability to cope with reality and a person's motivation to grow as a adult. This is a culture that sees drug use and trafficking as a viable economic reality. This lifestyle is glorified in popular hip hop and rap music and normalized in society. However, the trick is to engage in this lifestyle without becoming addicted, arrested, spending your life in jail, or getting killed. Not very good odds, considering the stronger penalties exacted by the criminal justice system on young Black males than those who are White, who also experiment with drugs. For many enterprising young men who want money in their pocket and street credibility, such an outcome is an acceptable risk.

- Joining a gang is a rite of passage experienced by many Black youth. I've watched a number of teenagers go to jail for the rest of their young lives because of involvement in serious crimes such as breaking and entering and drive-by shootings or other illicit gang activity. Some kids join gangs for safety's sake, for protection from rival gangs. Others join to belong to a community, a family they can call their own. For many teens they have no choice in the matter. Being part of a gang is a family affair; they were literally born into it. One's family is literally all in the gang, males and females, aunts and uncles, moms and dads. Whatever the reason, the consequences can be devastating.

Consider Von. He was big for his age as a preteen with a tough demeanor, and unfortunately that can draw the wrong kind of attention in our neighborhood. We were just beginning to develop a mentoring relationship; he loved to go to camp with Christ's Children. Unfortunately another group, older gang-related boys, appeared to want to "mentor" him as well. He began running around with them.

One day, Von was asked to jump in the car while they went to "take care of some business." Little did he know that the business involved retaliation for a shooting that happened earlier in the week. These boys attacked and killed someone. Von was unaware until the deed was done. Though significantly younger than the others, he received the harshest penalty because his running buddies made him the scapegoat. Lured by peer pressure and a desire to belong, Von got caught up in circumstances he could not control. There was no lawyer to look out for him, no advocate among his peers, no mercy within the system. He was sentenced to life in prison. This is the reality for too many boys in this demographic. Seemingly innocent situations and decisions can turn terribly wrong in an instant. Their environment necessitates constant vigilance and wariness of their peers and of their environment.

How does a nice, friendly, fun boy change into a hardened criminal? Von, like many others, was not a "gangsta" or "thug" type; he was a nice kid. But he grew up in an environment wherein the taboos of the larger mainstream society are irrelevant to his daily existence. For kids like Von there is a void in their lives where the positive guidance of a father should be. To people who are struggling to survive and have their basic needs met from day to day, the values that mainstream society hold as important do not carry very much weight.

Crime becomes an acceptable means to get what you need. If what you need is respect and recognition, and hurting someone else or violating their basic rights as an individual is all that stands in your way, it may be an acceptable trade. You don't do it because you're mean or evil; you just need what you need, and this is the only way you know how to get it. Sometimes, like Von, you don't even know what you're doing, or the consequences of said behavior.

Another rite of passage for this population includes living on the street or shacking up (cohabiting) with a woman who will support you and your bad behaviors or habits. An alarming phenomenon I've noticed is that of eighteen- and nineteen-year-old men living as partners with single mothers ten years their senior. Or if you get a girl pregnant with your children, you can live with your baby mama. *She* can get medical and housing assistance. For many young men, when you have achieved this, you've arrived. *You* are a man.

ROLE MODELS

Back to Terry. For Terry and me, our fathers played significant roles in learning what it meant to be a man and knowing when we had achieved that level of maturity. However, when there is no father or another positive male role model in the picture, there are other images of manhood that boys and teens in urban neighborhoods may model:

- There is the drug dealer, who is noticed by everyone. He's driving around in a nice automobile, aka a pimped-out whip with expensive rims on his tires. He rolls down the street, the bass on his car stereo thumping outrageously, making the windows on people's houses vibrate to the beat of the music. All the kids look up to him because he has money, possessions, and respect in the hood.
- There are the men who hang out at the corner or in front of the neighborhood store or on the front steps of apartment buildings. They may be drinking beer out of a brown paper sack, smoking blunts, cussing up a storm, and talking loud as they vent their anger against the White man and a system that keeps them down and won't let them get ahead. One day, driving through the neighborhood, I observed such a crowd of men coaxing two young boys to fight,

promoting the dangerous code of the streets that says you better knock someone else down before they knock you down.

- And remember the gangsters! Everything from the young men on the corner or in the street selling crack rocks or bags of marijuana, to the young wannabes and gangbangers runnin' around shooting up the neighborhood, to the real gangsters who control the streets from up in jail—middle-aged men confined behind bars—yet controlling and organizing crime in depressed neighborhoods.

- And don't forget! The absentee father leaves a legacy behind for young boys to emulate. Dad's absence speaks volumes in terms of what manhood means as it relates to family.

These are all, of course, negative models of manhood in depressed urban communities, but they are there for children to see. These are the ones we hear about the most when talking about problems facing Black families.

Nevertheless, there are other role models in poor urban communities who demonstrate much needed positive images of manhood. There are men like Terry's dad, who although he struggled with drug addiction, managed to teach his son what was right (incidentally, he overcame his addiction). There are single-parent families headed by men. In these circumstances, it may have been the mother who was overcome with drug addiction or some other problem and ended up leaving the family, and it was the father who stayed. These men have to fight uphill battles to keep their children, qualify for assistance from the government, and simply be trusted when they try to demonstrate that as a father, they love their children and will not give them up.

There are men like my dad, who are not very demonstrative in their nurturing or caring, but work very hard at all hours of the day to provide for the needs of the family—because they love their children. I know personally of one father in our ministry community who has been in and out of jail for most of his son's life. He does not live with his son and his son's mother, but since he has been out of jail, he has taken every opportunity to be with his son and encourage him to not make the same mistakes he did. As much as we note the problem of absentee fathers and a lack of positive role models for Black boys, we must recognize that there are some men out there doing what they are supposed to do, as best they can do it.

> **The absence of fathers and positive men can be a serious detriment to an individual or family. Conversely, the presence of positive male role models has a significant impact.**

The absence of fathers and positive men can be a serious detriment to an individual or family. Conversely, the presence of positive male role models has a significant impact. They are often overlooked, yet quietly exert tremendous influence every day. Married or unmarried, they live at home with their children and the children's mother, do their best to raise their children, get up out of bed and go to work, and stay in school and graduate; they are the pillars of the community. There are men who may not live with their children for various reasons, or men who are extended family or just family friends who put in extraordinary effort to guide and nurture the children in their lives.

According to a 2013 study of the Centers for Disease Control, Black men were found to be more involved in their children's lives than White or Hispanic fathers. Being perfect and not making mistakes are not the prerequisites of being a father or role model who may positively impact children. Being present, available, and involved in young people's lives is what counts.

In 1999, through the ministry of Dr. Arthur Rouner and the Pilgrim Center for Reconciliation, I was able to fulfill a lifelong dream of visiting the African continent as part of a team with World Vision Africa. World Vision Africa collaborated with the Pilgrim Center in supporting communities through engendering self-sufficiency in rural areas of East Africa through spiritual support and providing access to potable water. In the course of our journey, we visited disparate homes and families in the slums of Nairobi, the bush of western Kenya, the rain forests of Uganda, and the mountains of Ethiopia. We were tremendously privileged to interact with the people of these various communities as they opened up their homes and shared their lives with us.

In Uganda, we visited the home of a young man who at eighteen was taking care of his family of three siblings. Their mother and father had both died from complications from AIDS and he had been given charge of the family since he was sixteen. Such a heavy weight of responsibility for a young person! World Vision had helped train him in marketable work skills so he could earn a living and support his family. Relative to affluent US standards, his family lived in poverty; in his community, however, they were considered well-off to have a roof over their heads and food to eat. The younger children were going to school and having their basic needs taken care of, and they had hope for the future. This last—hope for the future—is something people in poverty in the US sorely lack. Though 45.8 percent of young Black children live in impoverished circumstances, compared to 14.5 percent of young White children, poverty in the US creates a psychological impact of hopelessness apart from availability of money and resources.[4]

I was tremendously impressed by the courage of this young man and his devotion to his family. It reminded me of a comparable situation back home: my young friend Dashawn, who is the oldest of three brothers. When their mother had left the family, they were young children, and their father had stepped in to raise them by himself. In subsequent years, the father had become an invalid due to health issues, and the three boys were basically raising themselves. Like that Ugandan boy, Dashawn stepped into the role of family leadership. The AIDS epidemic in East Africa has left millions of young children parentless. Many boys and girls have had to grow up quickly to assume parental roles for younger family members. In America, poor families in urban areas are facing an epidemic of sorts, a public health crisis in which too many Black children are growing up without fathers. Who knows what the continuing impact on mainstream American culture and on the Black community in particular will be?

BECOMING GOD'S MAN

No one wants to stay a child forever. Black males in urban communities most certainly do not. They hunger for significance and substance. They are crying out, "How do I know when I am a man? Somebody tell me! Somebody show me! Show me what a man looks like!" They respond to whoever shows up and demonstrates a lasting commitment (or even a passing interest, as with Von).

Two decades ago, I created a rites of passage program for use in our ministry: *Young Lions: Christian Rites of Passage for African American Young Men*. Published in 2000, it is designed to help young Black boys in experiencing and working through various levels of expectations to becoming a man. Mentor contact with Christian Black men and hands-on involvement are a critical part of the *Young Lions* curriculum. Youth are taught Christian values that encompass spiritual and cultural mores. As a group, spiritual, emotional, and social needs are addressed, including personal hygiene, human sexuality, work habits, self-concept and self-esteem, knowledge of African American heritage, culture, and the importance of education. The curriculum engages boys in positive interaction with African American men in preparation for adolescence and adulthood, helping to fulfill the need for positive male role models for boys who have none and reinforcing the image of positive Black manhood for those whose fathers are present.

The goal of *Young Lions* is to teach Black boys what it means to be African American men spiritually, culturally, and physically and to help teach them who they are in Christ. These three dimensions of self are explored thoroughly in order to infuse the boys with a strong self-image and self-esteem. With the curriculum as a help, leaders teach them that they are precious and valuable to God just as they are, that their Blackness comes from God and that God is the author of Blackness, that they can neither be truly Black nor truly a man apart from God. As it explores and affirms the innate spirituality and moral fiber of African American culture, the *Young Lions* program addresses the experience of Black boys from the holistic perspective of Christian ministry, providing positive experiences and dialogue about African American culture, heritage, and traditions. The *Young Lions* process provides an affirming atmosphere to examine the social and emotional aspects of daily life peculiar to the experience of Black boys. Most importantly, the gospel of Jesus Christ is communicated in a manner relevant to the experience of African American boys.

The role of Black men in a rites of passage program directed toward the needs of young Black boys and teens is vitally important. A Christian rites of passage should address problematic issues facing Black boys from the perspective of Christian Black men, who are uniquely suited to address them with these foundational premises. Through *Young Lions*, Black boys growing up in the inner city will

- see a better life for themselves when they see Black men modeling it for them;
- be naturally drawn to strong, firm, caring, and self-assured Black men, who show a genuine interest in them;
- become more equipped to survive and thrive as they learn and embrace who they are in Christ.

Positive male leadership is a critical component contributing to the development of male children. Rites of passage programs can provide a medium for Black boys to receive instruction from positive Black men, which can result in lives of realized potential and personal satisfaction.

The aim of *Young Lions*, in particular, is to cultivate and develop the inner person. Part of the methodology is to put nurturing Black men in a position to teach Black boys for the purpose of instilling hope for who they can be. The hope is that boys will internalize positive Christian beliefs about who they are in the world and their inherent value as creations of God, helping them to gain and possess inner peace and strength that can be brought to bear on their external situation, whatever it might be. Following the model of Jesus's boyhood, *Young Lions* is a program helping boys to grow "in wisdom and years, and in favor with God and with people" (Luke 2:52). The feedback, including from people who stop me on the street, programming that has sprung up around the country, and the relationships engendered, testifies to the impact and importance of helping this demographic to discover the path to becoming a man.

Before we run, we must walk. Before we walk, we must stand. Before one can be a man, he must have the opportunity to be a child. Before children can be adults, they must first learn and grow as children. The innocence of childhood is often the first casualty in the war that is impoverishment in America. Poor families endure so much stress that often the capacity to nurture the young is crowded out by the need to survive. Discipline, respect, and, most of all, love, are principles that are learned as children in the context of affirming families.

By teaching young Black boys that they are first children of God, they may see that they do have community and connection with others in the family of God. And God, by virtue of being God, will never forsake them or let them down, because God is their Father, Mother, everything they need. They can learn what they need to know about being human and being parents from God. As the psalmist said, "Even if my father and mother left me all alone, / the LORD would take me in" (Psalm 27:10). God will show the path to manhood. God will supply what is lacking in a young person's growing up so that he can begin the path to becoming a man. The apostle Paul said, "When I was a child, I spoke like a child, I thought like a child, I reasoned like a child; when I became an adult, I put an end to childish ways" (1 Corinthians 13:11 NRSV). When boys learn who they are in Christ, the question of manhood will not be answered by the preying forces of social and spiritual decay. They will grow and mature into men of God.

CHAPTER THREE
A GODLY MAN

When they are first getting to know me, kids in the neighborhood don't know what to make of me. When I speak grammatically correct English, they think I sound "White." They think I'm not cool because I don't spend a lot of money on the latest shoes. They think I'm rich because I own my own house. In these and many ways, they just can't relate to my image of Black manhood. In their experience, this is not what a Black man looks like. One time, while driving around taking kids home, I was talking with them about substance abuse and drugs. During our conversation I told them that I had never tried drugs or even smoked cigarettes. They flat out did not believe me. "C'mon Chris, never?" "No, I never have," I insisted. "Sure, Chris," they said—in a way that I knew they didn't believe me. But as we spent more and more time together and as they observed my lifestyle and faith, they began to accept what I said about myself to be fact, however strange and foreign to them.

And don't even bring up sex. Whenever it comes up that I was a virgin until I got married at twenty-nine, they really lose their minds. I still don't know if they really believe me on that one. They also could not believe that I don't, as a rule, lie. They ask me:

- Chris, how come you got married?
- Didn't you ever smoke marijuana?
- How could you ever go that long before you had sex with a girl?

And my answer is always the same: I became a Christian when I was thirteen and since then I've been trying to live my life the way God wants me to. I don't know then if they feel really sorry for me or if they are impressed, but they just shake their heads and almost sadly reply, "Wow!"

When I was about nine years old, my family lived in Tuskegee, Alabama. We lived right down the street from the local United Methodist church, which my family attended. My best friend was Artie, and his dad was the pastor. I really looked up to Artie's dad and viewed him with reverence. At one Sunday service, Artie's dad asked people to come forward who wanted to be baptized. Artie and I went forward. When I got home and told my mom, she informed me that I had been baptized as a baby at another church. I had not been aware of this fact. Nevertheless, at this point in my life, I made a decision for myself to be consecrated to and set apart for God. Artie's dad represented reverent holiness to me. He was a minister and a servant of God; he was approachable because he was my best friend's dad. This was my first strong image of a godly man. Holy and approachable, someone to whom I could relate. I'm sure my contact with him was a significant factor in my seeking Christ and becoming a minister myself.

The toughest guy I ever knew growing up is my dad. (He still is!) He was tough because he'd made a career as a military soldier and had risen through the ranks to the highest position a noncommissioned soldier could achieve, Command Sergeant Major. As a child, I often thought he was mean because he was very disciplined in raising his children. My dad was a God-fearing person, and he and my mom raised us in the Church. I never witnessed my dad behaving in a way detrimental toward his wife or kids. I remember when I was little, waking up at five in the morning and hearing my mom and dad in the kitchen. He was going to work and she was making him breakfast. I went back to sleep feeling sorry for my dad, who had to get up early every day to go to work, and I wouldn't see him until dinnertime. But as I dozed off, I realized that he did it for his family. Such memories have stuck with me and helped to shape me into the man I am today. From my dad, I learned discipline in life, the value of hard work, and commitment and devotion to family.

When he was forty, my older brother, Tyrone, died from a brain tumor, but really his life, as I knew it, ended many years earlier as a result of a drug overdose. I had always looked up to him. He was a talented athlete, popular at school, and tough and streetwise. He always looked out for me and my brothers. We lived in a rough neighborhood, but no one ever messed with us when they found out Tyrone was our brother. He had an opportunity to play basketball at a Division I school, but fell in with a bad crowd and began a downward spiral that led him away from our family and into the streets. Heroin abuse destroyed his mind and when my parents found him, he was living on the streets in New York City. No one ever spoke ill of him in my family, but his life acted as a cautionary tale—what not to do. He, my dad, and Artie's dad were the primary images of manhood that stayed with me as I grew up.

LIVING RIGHTEOUSLY

What does a godly man look like? For me, the term *godly* means "being like God" or being righteous—that is, right with God. Philippians 3:9 teaches that no one is righteous by his or her own power but we are to seek the righteousness that comes from God through faith in Christ Jesus. A righteous or godly man pleases God by living according to God's Word, obeying God's commandment by faith. It is rare to see a person who is consistently living this way in any venue of our society. Young Black males need to witness and have access to the lives of Christian men who are living righteously. Bear in mind, I am not talking about simply having good behavior such as being nice or going to church every Sunday, but someone who demonstrates Christian character and daily obedience to Christ's teachings in their conduct and relationships.

My wife and I raised our kids here in Minneapolis, in a rough neighborhood. We dealt constantly with drugs, gangs, shootings, and other neighborhood turmoil. Developing relationships with our neighbors was difficult because our block had lots of rental units and people moved around frequently. I was active in the community and known for my work with boys in the neighborhood. I was often called upon to settle disputes between boys or young men that were apt to become violent. There were frequent skirmishes right in front of our house over issues of turf, gang loyalties, and stolen possessions.

One afternoon there was a ruckus involving local boys, most of whom I knew. I went outside and broke up the fight. Most of the kids listened to me and settled down. One boy, however, didn't see why they should stop fighting just on my say-so. He didn't know me. To him I was just some grown-up butting into his business. While none of the others would follow his lead to make more trouble, he refused to listen and leave. At that moment, his aunt happened to come by and soundly rebuked him for making trouble. Following his aunt home, he exasperatedly asked her, "Who is that man, Auntie?" She said, "That's Pastor Chris, boy!"

This event demonstrates the importance of relationship and investing in a community over a long period of time. Unless I had done the groundwork of building relationships, building a solid reputation in the community, I might well have come to harm that day. Incarnational ministry of this sort, living among people and sharing their struggles and successes, is the surest way of developing genuine, redemptive relationships with urban residents.

I am always gratified when I speak to parents or young people and they tell me they've heard of or know of me. It makes me feel like what we're doing is working. They have a nephew who went to camp with me; I did the funeral of their cousin; I visited their father when he was in prison; and so on. I'm both humbled and fearful because it reminds me that people are watching. I've earned their respect and my opinion means something, not because I live a perfect life, but because of my transparency. People can see who I really am; I am not pretending to be something I'm not. I work hard to be genuine and accessible. They listen to me because they see that I am committed. They relate to the fact that my family has suffered from the same community distress that they do. People from outside the community, like teachers, may work and have great impact on inner-city children and families; but the greatest impact by far is by those who share the experiences of suffering and stress by living in the community.

My neighbors trust me because I've stood with them through hard times and good. I've been blessed by the Lord's grace not to have made any major dumb mistakes that may tarnish my reputation in the community. But while I attribute this to God's grace, simply another tool for God to use to reveal God's self to people here, I can't afford not to use my life as an example. I take advantage of the goodwill and reputation I have sown and built up over the years to lift up Christ and challenge people to live for God. My words and testimony of Christ's goodness and faithfulness ring of personally experienced truth and the conviction of a faith that is tried, tested, and proven. Through my life, relationships, and ministry, I say as the apostle Paul did, "Follow my example, just like I follow Christ's" (1 Corinthians 11:1).

What I pray for in our ministry is that the Lord will allow us to cultivate and develop young men to be followers of Christ that they might seed this community and replicate what I am doing, influencing whomever they may. In this community, I want to create in young Black men a passion for Christ and concern for others. I frequently receive comments from other ministers, parents in the community, teachers at schools where I volunteer: "I wish you could clone yourself" or "Too bad you can't multiply yourself." In essence, that is what we are trying to do. However, what is really needed is not a clone of Chris McNair but something that has tremendous potential for impacting and changing an urban community for the better—Black men who know who they are in Christ.

MORALITY VS. SPIRITUALITY

There were two groups of people who most influenced my social life at a Christian college in West Texas. The first was a group of upperclassmen who were on a ministerial track of studies, as I was. They were excited about their faith and ready to share it with anyone at any time or place. One guy in particular impressed me as a Christian leader. His devotion and charisma were different (more vibrant, exuberant, enthusiastic) from what I was used to in the churches I had attended growing up. Apart from Christian fellowship, I was also involved with sports: track and field and basketball. The second group was my sports friends, not very religious. They didn't attend church or participate in campus Christian fellowship activities. They didn't appear to be very moral but they possessed a deep spirituality. I learned a lot about being a Christian from them. Most of the students in the first group I described were White, whereas most of the second group were Black. At our school and in the region, Black and White people did not mix. Whites were afraid of Blacks, and Blacks found White people to be untrustworthy. Sadly, the White Christians, who were part of a great majority, fell right in line with this social status quo. They would not associate with, talk about Jesus to, or hang out with Black people. My sports friends saw this behavior as being hypocritical and fake.

One day in the locker room, one of my athlete friends told me just that: "Your White Christian friends are fake!" I took issue with that statement, saying, "You don't know what you're talking about!" After a heated discussion, he told me that on several occasions, he'd seen my charismatic friend, the one whom I admired so, getting drunk and carousing at local clubs. I didn't believe him. It couldn't be true! From all appearances, this young man was a strong Christian; he was a powerful role model for me. But I learned something that day because it turned out that my friend had feet of clay. Just because a person looks, talks, and even acts like a Christian in some ways doesn't mean that person is a Christian. Someone said to me once, "A Christian is someone who turns out to be one." When I first heard that statement, I thought it was mumbo jumbo, but over the years I've grown to appreciate the veracity of that adage/proverb. Every day each of us must make choices about whether or not to live for Christ. It is *not* what we say; it is what we *do* that matters.

What does a godly man look like? A godly man should exhibit Christian values and behaviors as described by the Bible. According to Galatians 5:16, a godly person must be "guided by the Spirit and you won't carry out your selfish desires." A godly person should exhibit the fruits of the Spirit: "love, joy, peace, patience, kindness, goodness, faithfulness, gentleness, and self-control" (Galatians 5:22-23). According to 2 Peter 1:4-7, faith, moral excellence, knowledge, self-control, endurance, godliness, affection for others, and love are additional characteristics of the life of a person seeking Christ and following God. Nevertheless, there are a few tensions that must be discussed here in regard to how the biblical mandate relates to historical and contemporary culture. Every day, young Black men growing up in the inner city are confronted with choices that on the surface seem to put their culture and Christian spirituality in conflict.

I have had opportunity to collaborate in an advisory capacity with a Christian ministry, stemming from a White, mainstream, evangelical culture, whose goal was to rehab housing in depressed neighborhoods and making housing available and affordable for poor people. This organization was run by people who had no experience of being poor or economically or racially oppressed. Their life experiences were diametrically opposed to the experiences of those among whom they were seeking to minister. Invariably conflict would arise over behavior, conduct, or rental agreements between poor Black tenants and their White and middle-class, albeit Christian, landlords. To the credit of the latter, they made sincere attempts to resolve conflicts in a manner sensitive to the experience of the poor. However, the issue that often broke the camel's back was a lack of honesty on the part of the tenant. Honesty or telling the truth became the litmus test for the character of a tenant. If a person was caught in a lie, then all efforts to build a relationship or work with that person ceased. It seemed like all thoughts of compassion or grace simply flew out of the window if a tenant was caught in the single transgression of lying. Love, it seemed, would cover a multitude of sins, but it wouldn't cover lying. The difficult thing to accept about this posture is that it demonstrates a lack of understanding of the realities of existence among poor people in urban communities.

From the days of slavery, oppressed Black people have had a different take on lying and stealing than the mainstream culture. How could a White person, who was stealing their very bodies, lives, labor, and even children, have a moral leg to stand on when accusing an enslaved person of stealing a pig or anything else? Jermain "Jarm" Wesley Loguen (1813–1872), in the course of escaping slavery, stole a horse from his master (who was also his father) and settled in New York. He later became a bishop in the African Methodist Episcopal Zion Church. Twenty-six years later when the widow Sarah Logue (his previous owner) found out where he was, she wrote and called him a thief, conduct unbecoming a preacher, and demanded payment for him and the horse in the amount of $1,000. He wrote back that should he send her money, it would be to purchase freedom for his siblings whom she and her husband had sold as their property. And furthermore, that should she attempt to re-enslave him, she would find out how fiercely he believed in his right to freedom; that he would use his strong right arm as well as those of his strong and brave friends. Jarm would fit right in here in the hood!

Bishop Loguen didn't think what he did was wrong; although technically, he lied, cheated, and stole. He believed he was justified in his behavior in order to escape slavery. In fact, his former mistress "owed" him that horse and much more because of the injustice perpetrated on him and his family. Lying and dishonesty are ingrained and acceptable behaviors practiced by many among the disenfranchised poor to deal with racist institutions and address basic needs and survive in a hostile environment. Being poor often engenders a fundamental lack of trust in institutions. Lying becomes a mechanism for coping and survival—indeed a default position, taken by the powerless against the powerful.

I have been on the receiving end of dishonest behavior many times, but I never let it become a relationship breaker. It is rather an opportunity to teach, learn, and grow with this person. Being taken advantage of is an occupational hazard of working in economically challenged communities. Compassion has always been the issue of overriding concern for me in these situations. If I was going to make a mistake, it would be for acting from a sense of compassion, not from a sense of rightness. Many times it seems like evangelical Christians, like the Pharisees of Jesus's time, are more intent on observing the letter of the law than keeping the intent of the law when it comes to biblical principles and mandates.

In today's world, the topic of ethics has become a subjective minefield with the polar values of what is right and what is wrong diffused by the area of grayness that separates them. There is hardly such a thing as an empirical ethical standard in human society anymore. Whatever feels good, whatever feels right: these are the values that guide human social behavior today. There seems to be no right or wrong, no moral absolute.

Many people have a situational concept of ethics. For those who are poor, the rightness or wrongness of an issue often depends on survival: "How can I feed my children?" "How can I provide shelter for my family?" Strict adherence to mainstream moral values gives way to the ongoing struggle to meet one's basic needs for food, shelter, and safety. The common value is, "You do what you have to to get by." Taken to the extreme, this sentiment means that lying and cheating become acceptable practices in order to get what is needed to survive. However, these practices are not unique to poor people. In mainstream culture, moral values are regularly sacrificed on the altar of affluence and power. The news is replete with scandals of mismanagement and misconduct among corporate CEOs and politicians in America. My parents often observed that lying, cheating, and stealing were condemned in America only if you are inept at it and get caught. If you are wealthy and engage in such behaviors, you are considered a shrewd businessman, but if you are poor, you are a criminal and a thief.

Spirituality supersedes morality. Spirituality in marginal communities is marked by a dependence on God's grace, not only for personal salvation in the face of one's own sinful nature, but for provision in a society intent on depriving your community. Many Christians who have grown up in oppressed and poor environments live with a peculiar tension between Christian spirituality and a lifestyle based on survival ethics. For the godly person, the moral quality of one's lifestyle corresponds to the level of faith one possesses that God is actively involved in their daily reality. I'm talking about those who live in circumstances where the struggle to have basic needs met is a constant stress and takes a toll on their well-being. Many urban Black males who live decent lifestyles would almost certainly be considered amoral by most mainstream Christians, because their values digress from traditionally accepted norms. Poor people live in a different reality than that of most mainstream Christians, regardless of ethnicity. Thus, the issue of survival plays a primary role in the spirituality of the unchurched poor.

Common examples of survival ethics not conforming to traditional moral standards include families in which

- parents have children but remain unmarried because the system has made it more fiscally viable for a single mother to receive aid;
- widowed seniors cohabit in order not to lose hard-earned benefits from deceased spouses;
- families defrauding utility companies, using their children's names in order to gain services, but thereby incurring greater debt and mortgaging their children's future;
- parents who may receive public assistance but hustle on the side, trying to make extra money through an extra job.

In their reality, misrepresenting the truth in order to negotiate bureaucratic social service systems becomes necessary sometimes to acquire basic needs. The evil of lying pales in comparison to that of potential eviction, hunger, or unemployment. In these situations and others, individuals may be trapped in extremely oppressive circumstances that warrant a certain street wisdom to survive. While these practices are condemned by mainstream society, communities of poor people see it as exercising common sense. Dishonesty and deception is an age-old technique used by weak and oppressed people to cope with their equally dishonest, deceptive, but stronger oppressors.

Our country's history supports this. From Frederick Douglass to Harriet Tubman, enslaved human beings would use every means, including theft and lying, by which to escape slavery and steal away to freedom. During Jim Crow days, Black people did not hesitate to "shine people on," to practice deception in order to avoid abuse and mistreatment. In an environment where the quality of life is held hostage by redlining and other institutional racist practices, resulting in the lack of basic physical, social, and emotional needs, the values of mainstream society just don't matter that much. It is not that the sins of lying, cheating, or stealing should be overlooked, but before condemning individuals in extreme circumstances, evangelical Christians cannot afford to be like the Pharisees who clamored to throw the first stone at the woman caught in adultery, a sin with shared guilt.

The spirituality of the poor is not perfect, but it helps people get through each day and provides some meaning to life. Their human nature is just as fundamentally depraved as that of the mainstream middle class. It is just as immoral, just as covetous, just as self-centered. Their spirituality does not condone immoral behavior, but it differs significantly in that it detests oppression and injustice. This is generally not true for the spirituality of the upper and middle class who often benefit from a system that oppresses others.

The spirituality of the urban poor affirms that God is sovereign, just, and merciful. No one thinks they will escape the judgment of God; but God is the judge, and God is full of wisdom, grace, and mercy. Like David when presented with his guilt by the prophet Gad (2 Samuel 24:14), from their experienced perspective, it is much better to be in the hands of God than in the hands of man. Many of the urban poor today have not had this spiritual heritage passed on to them from their families or communities. They are thus relegated to living to survive from day to day, getting what they need from anyone they can, however they can, without even knowledge of God's grace and love to temper an often unbearable existence.

HONESTY AND SINCERITY

One of the hazards of incarnational ministry in the city is the experience of a home burglary. It was bad enough when a neighbor broke into our house, but on a few instances, a trusted young friend stole from us. It was most painful when someone we welcomed into our home stole from us. In particular, there was one young man we had known from an early age and was in our core group of kids; he stole some money from us. The broken trust, dishonesty, and disregard of relationship was painful to bear, but I worked to stay in relationship with him. What was especially ironic is that he could have asked us for anything and we would've helped him. Having been caught he didn't want to be around me and couldn't see how I could still want to be friends with him. There were consequences to his behavior but we succeeded in repairing the relationship. Nevertheless, to this day he has not been able to shake off the shackles of abuse and deprivation that marred him at an early age and evoked the desperation in him that caused him to steal from us in the first place. There is hope though, and we remain committed to helping him move forward in his life.

There is no crime in making a mistake. It should not ruin a young person's life! But if you are young, Black, male, and poor, one mistake *can* ruin your life—if not kill you. A young Black male cannot overlook or forget the fates of Jamar Clark and more than ninety other Black men who have been killed by police in recent years. The rate of incarceration of young Black men for minor crimes as compared to young White men is frightening. I spend an inordinate amount of time trying to instill this into the thinking of young men in my community. All it takes is one misstep, one angry outburst, one uncontrolled or irresponsible action to result in a school expulsion, a loss of job, a prison sentence, or the worst of all, extreme violence resulting in death from police brutality, street violence, and other inner-city hazards. Black men have to know how to work the system, a system that is rigged to work against them. They have to be "wise as serpents and innocent as doves," keeping their emotions in check because just as Jesus said, they are out there among wolves (Matthew 10:16 NRSV). They have to be careful because in our society they are targets of injustice and institutional racism and may unwittingly start a chain of events that can ruin their lives. In my experience as a Black man, the best way to beat the system is to transcend it. Give yourself to a system, an order, which transcends this world.

I submit that a godly man, one who is following the dictates of Christ in his daily living, is going to stand apart in this world—whether that person is a part of mainstream America or among the urban poor. Howard Thurman, the author of *Jesus and the Disinherited*, addresses this issue. Into this morass of ethics and survival Thurman raises the issue of honesty, being truthful and sincere. When Thurman talks about honesty and sincerity, or the lack thereof among the urban poor, he does not define it as simply telling the truth, or refraining from telling falsehoods, but as being true to God and one's self. "Sincerity in human relations is equal to, and the same as, sincerity to God. . . . Man's relation to man and man's relation to God are one relation."[1] Being poor in America is an extreme condition, constantly challenging one's sense of personhood and morality. People in extreme circumstances often find themselves required to do extreme things in order to work them out. Moral and ethical considerations often come second to survival, meeting one's basic needs, when one is in poverty. No matter the extremity of the situation, Thurman points to the model of Jesus Christ as the path of empowerment for the poor and disinherited. Christ did not excuse situational or survival ethics, although he himself was poor. He advocated honesty not for the sake of adhering to societal mores; rather, he called people to a higher standard of being honest before God. Honesty was a value he espoused not for personal gain or reward, or even because God would reward the one who did the right thing toward his neighbor; but as a quality characteristic of life and relationship with God. For Christ, being honest before God was more important than temporary physical needs.

People need to live for something more than just survival. The model Christ taught and lived out was the model of being honest, obedient before God, even to the point of death. Christ equated being honest in human relationships with honesty with God. Christ modeled an attitude of holy honesty, which was borne not from a sense of *oughtness*, but engendered through a relationship with God. There are worse things than going hungry. There are worse things than doing without material needs or even being put out in the street. The prospect of falling out of relationship with God puts survival ethics into perspective. For human beings driven by the instinct to survive, it is the only thing that puts survival in the back seat.

With this conviction a young man may take the risk of being truthful. There is no crime in making a mistake. Even if the mistake itself is a crime, there are ways to overcome it. With the proper support, a young person may overcome many personal, social, or legal troubles. If mistakes are made, a person must be forthcoming and honest about them, whether it is lying on an application, betraying someone's trust, or a moment of bad judgment. The old adage that it is always better if you tell the truth actually has some veracity. When young men encounter people of good will and act in good faith, the chances are good that telling the truth about a modest criminal record or experience with drugs will not negatively impact them. Many employers are willing to give them a chance to prove their reliability and faithfulness.

The godly man is honest. He is honest in the sense that he lives his life according to the only truth there is: that of the reality of Jesus Christ. Everything else is transitory. All things, in this world and the next, are subservient to Christ, the truth of his existence. How this plays out practically is for the individual to see one's self as truly being a "new creation" in Christ (2 Corinthians 5:17) and not of this world nor subject to the mores of this world. The old has gone, the new has come! The man of God does not have to play the world's games or submit to the world's ideologies; he is living in a new paradigm, that of God's kingdom. Practicing honesty under the most extreme circumstances elevates one to the presence of God. If we give up our sinful, albeit socially acceptable, ways to trust in God's providence, God will demonstrate faithfulness. We will assert, like the psalmist, "I have never seen the righteous left all alone, / have never seen their children begging for bread" (Psalm 37:25). The man or woman who learns to trust God has overcome the world. The godly man can transcend not only the physical limitations of this life, but the human moral assignations as well because he lives by a higher standard—that of the life of Christ. The godly man has a higher calling than survival; his calling is to live for Christ.

HOPE AND HEALING

Effective Christian ministry to young people disseminates hope and compassion. This ministry is manifested through a great deal of love, a lot of pain, and little return. The specific goal of ministry among the urban poor is not simply to address needs but to instill hope by surrounding the disenfranchised and socially isolated poor with a loving, caring, and empowering community of relationships. The spiritual condition of hopelessness is the greatest obstacle to genuine Christian community and personal fulfillment. Hopelessness leads to chemical abuse, crime and violent behavior, and immorality. A fundamental lack of self-worth and self-esteem due to malignant, lingering poverty or institutional ostracism is at the root of antisocial and self-destructive behavior. Imparting the gospel of hope and compassion requires personal identification and consistent involvement through personal, redemptive relationships. The gospel of Christ promises eternal life through forgiveness of sins; but Christ also promises abundant life in the here and now (John 10:10 NRSV). Young people need hope for today and tomorrow, the promise of abundant life here on earth.

The urban poor are hurting people in need of healing. They exhibit a heightened sensitivity to relationships due to betrayal, mistrust, and various forms of social discrimination and neglect. Too often, Black males in the city are treated as renegades and pariahs. Many of them have developed a dysfunctional social structure and a way of relating to people that hinders them from accepting Christian community and connecting to God through fellowship within the body of Christ. And yet, this is exactly what is needed. The connection of personal relationships with supportive Christians for prayer, encouragement, and even simple conversation creates a sense of Christian community that signifies that each person is important and precious to God. Acceptance and grace in the context of human relationships provide healing and hope. So the concept of forgiveness is a critical issue. Receiving God's forgiveness and learning to forgive others who have wronged them provide empowerment to deal with the oppressive realities of everyday life. This kind of healing does not occur instantaneously (for some it does not occur at all); but experiencing acceptance and grace enables one to persevere and brings hope for eternal justice and peace.

> **The godly man realizes that he is a spiritual being and that as a Black man he has a rich heritage on which to rely, a historical and contemporary presence of Black men standing up for what is right, even at the cost of personal comfort.**

A GODLY MAN

What does a godly man look like to young Black men who have little hope in themselves, their community, or society at large; who have no trust in personal relationships or public institutions due to debilitating stress and institutional racism? How is the Christian gospel an influence? How can the Christian gospel assuage this sense of hopelessness?

Urban youth need to see godly men in their communities, modeling the hope of Christ.

A godly man is moral. He seeks to live by codes of biblical righteousness as lived out by men in his community who refuse to give in to temptations for the quick fix, that temporary high, quick and easy cash money, and/or attempts to manipulate the system. The godly man works to improve himself and those around him, such as men who are going to school, working a job, and raising their children.

A godly man is spiritual. He adheres to a set of values higher than those exhibited in the societies of the world, whether in the hood or in the mainstream, striving to live according to the teachings of Jesus Christ. He seeks first the kingdom of God and its righteousness, trusting that everything else will fall into place (Matthew 6:33). The godly man realizes that he is a spiritual being and that as a Black man he has a rich heritage on which to rely, a historical and contemporary presence of Black men standing up for what is right, even at the cost of personal comfort. Young people need to see that there is a set of values that is higher than this world's and seek to come in line with God's will.

51

A godly man is honest. He is committed to being true to self and God, regardless of differing standards all around. Youth must see men who are honest, not as a capitulation to the societal mores of the mainstream that has ostracized them, but out of respect and obedience to the God who made them, loves them, and calls them to a higher standard. A Black man must respond to the call of God on his life to walk his own path to glory.

A godly man is hopeful. He has put his hope in something beyond himself and his world. He can see beyond his present circumstance into a better future for himself, his family, and his community. He gets this hope from God because to hope only in ourselves is a false hope. Human beings are part of the problem; all the ills of this world stem from humanity's separation from God. Our sinful nature, our rebellion against what God wants, our focus on self—these are all earmarks of human nature; they are the roots of problematic issues faced in every segment of human society, Black, White, young, old, male, or female. However, God through Jesus Christ has intervened that all may be forgiven of their sins and enter into right relationship with God. The godly man hopes in God. He depends on a power outside of the social construct of humankind, counting on God to make it through every moment of each day. With the psalmist he says, "Do I have anyone else in heaven? / There's nothing on earth I desire except you" (Psalm 73:25).

The godly man is a stranger in a strange land, yearning to go home. He knows that home is more than clothing, shelter, and social status. He has a home beyond his present circumstance. The godly man looks to Christ to meet issues or needs involving family, relationships, money, food, and shelter. His hope is in Christ alone; he trusts in Christ for every need, knowing that in Christ, he not only has "righteousness and sanctification and redemption" (1 Corinthians 1:30 NRSV), but also has everything needed for spiritual or physical needs (Philippians 4:19).

Sometimes, things don't go the way we need them to. And when they go badly, we are sure that God does not see us. A young man in my group, who is active in our sports teams, retreats, and other activities, professed his faith in God and came to Christ one summer. That fall, his family went through some financial struggles and he claimed that he ceased to believe in God. When I asked him why, he said, "Because when I needed God to help me, he wasn't there." A few months later he was walking home with his friends from a party. Someone they had offended at the party drove past them shooting, intent on killing them. One of his friends got grazed by a bullet on the cheek, another was shot in the arm, and he was struck by a bullet that went through his thigh, without hitting an artery or any bones. They all recovered quickly. When I spoke to him in the hospital I reminded him of what he had said. "It turns out God was there for you after all, huh?" I said. He sheepishly agreed. Christian believers who grow up in the city like this young man must learn to trust God through hard times as well as good. They must learn that God is always there for them, even when they are in crisis.

Young men struggle with being a man in the world; they wonder how concepts of godly living work. How do they know the right thing to do when what may seem situationally correct conflicts with what is modeled by Jesus Christ and godly people they respect? It comes down to trust and faith, commitment and obedience. But everyone has moments of doubt. When John Wesley doubted his own faith, he was advised by a colleague, Peter Boehler, "Preach faith till you have it; and then, because you have it, you will preach faith."[2] Similarly, my counsel for Black men is this: live righteously because you love God, and because you love God, you will live righteously. A godly man must be able to trust that God is with him always, as promised in Hebrews 13:5. When bad things happen, God is right there with us. Youth must learn through experience that God may not deliver them from all trouble, but God will always be there when they need him.

Trusting in anything is a great risk for people whose trust has been betrayed and abused in the past. But the call of discipleship requires no less than for Black males among the urban poor to put their trust in Christ, who will not let them down. Complete dependence on God may be frightening, especially to those whose sense of manhood includes non-dependence and being in control. Nevertheless, the only lasting sense of hope can come when one takes that step of complete trust to experience the all-encompassing security of being in God's hands. A godly man puts his hope in Christ, becoming utterly dependent upon him. He knows that he is not alone, that God has not forsaken him. The answer to the hopelessness experienced by many youth in urban communities is to introduce them to the hope that will not disappoint. "Hope does not disappoint us, because God's love has been poured into our hearts through the Holy Spirit that has been given to us" (Romans 5:5 NRSV).

CHAPTER FOUR

A CHRISTIAN IN THE HOOD

One afternoon I went to visit one of the families in our parish. They lived in a part of the neighborhood in which there were actively disputed gang boundaries. Upon arrival, their teenaged son, Martice, was on the front steps talking with friends from the block. I hung out with them for a while, listening to an odd discussion about which fast-food joint was better: Burger King, McDonald's, or Dairy Queen. When I'd heard enough, I asked Martice if he wanted to go get something to eat. We left. In the car, when I asked why they were having such an intense conversation about something as trivial as fast food, he started laughing. He explained that they weren't talking about food, but about gang loyalties: the Disciples, the Bloods, and the Crips. I felt stupid. I asked, "What if somebody really thought you were just talking about food and jumped into the conversation and said, 'I love McDonald's'?" He said, "If it was you, nothing would happen, they'd probably just laugh. But if it was me, I'd get jumped."

55

At one point in time, there were six incidents of shootings and murders near Martice's house; his block had become a war zone. I went over to see how he was holding up and asked, "When stuff like this happens, don't you get scared? What do you do?" He said, "Of course I get scared! I stay in the house. I don't associate with anybody. When I want to go out, I go to the gym [less than a block from his house]. And when I'm done playing basketball, I come right back home." Unless someone from our ministry picks him up for an activity, he stays in the house. Once I had to drop him off a block away from his house. He jumped out of the van and sped down the street and didn't slow down until he was on his porch. This is the way he survives.

Martice had given his life to Christ at camp the year before. Before becoming a Christian, Martice was tightly wound up with stress and fear. Confessing his sins or trusting Jesus to give him eternal life was not an obstacle to him becoming a Christian. But he was afraid that if he became a Christian, he'd be too soft to protect his family: his mom from her boyfriend, his siblings from neighborhood thugs. He said, with tears running down his cheeks, "I don't want to hurt anybody. But if he touches my mom again, we're gonna fight. Somebody's going to get hurt. I don't want to hurt anybody. But if someone on the corner steps up to my sister or one of my little brothers, I'm going to hurt somebody."

After releasing this burden of stress and fear to the Lord, Martice accepted Christ and his life has changed. He still lives in the same environment, but he is not consumed with fear. He has friends his age in our church and he enjoys various activities. He has me and others in our church with whom to share his burdens. He trusts God to protect his family. He is enjoying his life as a teenager and trying to live in a way that pleases God.

These circumstances remind me of how different daily life is for Black males growing up in the hood, how having the right information is paramount to survival: to keep from being jumped, beat down, stolen from, punked, beat up, or worse. To insure protection for himself and his family, a young man must cultivate hardness, as well as a reputation that he will get crazy in order to preserve his due respect. To negotiate these streets, kids have to know where gang boundaries are, what colors to wear or not wear, which park or block is safe, and which fast-food joint to which to claim loyalty. The specifics may differ depending on locale, but the dynamics are the same.

Kids rarely go more than a few blocks away from their home for fear of being attacked or being held up at gunpoint. It is sobering to consider that they have to be so careful in their speech, expressions, and actions, that their very welfare depends on their knowledge of street culture. They must find ways to fit in and not draw attention to themselves or be more crazy and feared than the neighborhood predators. They must be well-versed in the protocol of the neighborhood and streets. In Minneapolis, for instance, over North they must be cognizant of when or whether they've crossed over from the "highs" to the "lows" (referring to street numbers); on the South Side, they must know whether they are in the neighborhoods of Central (Rolling 30s Bloods) or Phillips (Native and Somali gangs), as well as understanding whose territory is what within those blocks. Is there any conflict between being streetwise and being a Christian in the hood? Many think it's impossible to be a Christian and be hard enough to survive in the hood. There are three tensions that must be taken into account for effective discipleship: peers, home, and relationships.

PEERS

The peer group is important in societies. The peer group is a primary group of people who have similar interests, age, background, and social status. Peer pressure is the influence that is felt among a peer group, which can be negative or positive. For young people, the peer group is the most influential and important group in their lives. Peer pressure outweighs any other influence, that of school, family, or church. It concerns the interplay between individuals and within the group that relates to the adoption of a *persona of coolness*, one's image in the hood, which is a primary coping mechanism.

To be cool means to keep emotions in check and not let on to others how one really feels. The streetwise male must adapt a particular attitude as a survival technique:

- Nothing bothers him, nothing excites him, nothing reaches him deeply. He feels nothing.
- He is carefully aloof and detached with no real friends, just associates.
- He often depersonalizes individuals, both male and female. He is not vulnerable.
- He never appears stressed, regardless of the circumstance or harsh realities.

The consequences of keeping one's feelings bottled up and never express-ing or releasing them are destructive. Behavioral conflict and violent tenden-cies in various settings such as the school or home may be traced to the tension of keeping strong feelings bottled up within. *The culture of detached cool* results in isolation for the individual. Black males become isolated from family, loved ones, and peers, and even become out of touch with themselves, as they deny their own strong feelings in order to avoid emotional pain. Although they may seem dominant and in charge, isolation from others and self is the price paid for cultivating coolness.

A related quality this peer group cultivates is to be hard. *Being hard* means doing whatever it takes to get what you need. You are prepared to go to any extreme to preserve your respect, and you don't take disrespect from anyone. If you have a reputation for being hard, people respect you. Someone who is hard

- portrays toughness, enduring any pain, emotional or physical;
- displays no vulnerability, rarely smiling or showing his true feelings;
- does not demonstrate that he cares deeply about anyone or anything;
- will go to any length to preserve his respect;
- is intently focused on survival, not swayed by relationships or circumstances.

Conflict with police, family, peers, anyone in authority—it's all the same. When you're hard, you are prepared for anything and you handle whatever comes up. Being hard is probably the most desirable quality among the street-wise; being hard isolates you from others because you don't need anyone or anything—you can make it on your own.

Men, in general, struggle with the need to appear strong and able to deal with anything. In our society, men are not encouraged to feel or express cer-tain feelings, or make themselves vulnerable by opening up to others. How-ever, this tension is exacerbated by poverty. In the constant struggle to have basic needs met, interpersonal relationships often suffer. Coping mechanisms such as being cool or hard become the strongest expressions of self. Letting one's guard down by exhibiting gentleness or compassion is contrary to the street ideals of manhood; to cultivate any gentle or vulnerable feelings is to risk losing respect.

> **Becoming a Christian requires vulnerability, a surrender to God. To grow as a disciple means abandoning all facades that block a deepening relationship with Christ and with others. One must become real, and being real means feeling and dealing with pain.**

What does it mean to be a Christian in the context of a culture of coolness and hardness? Becoming a Christian requires vulnerability, a surrender to God. To grow as a disciple means abandoning all facades that block a deepening relationship with Christ and with others. One must become real, and being real means feeling and dealing with pain. Showing vulnerability and/or revealing strong feelings is not cool; it is construed as a sign of weakness. However, in order to grow in Christ, Black males must learn as the apostle Paul did that "when I'm weak, then I'm strong" (2 Corinthians 12:10).

The story of Mookie, a young man whom I have known for years, from running around the neighborhood as a boy to becoming a positive role model as a man, illustrates this point. Active in our youth programs and in our church, he lived in an environment that often called his Christian values into question. In order to survive among peers and family dysfunction, he often adopted a persona of coolness and of being hard. In spite of this, he grew as a Christian and became a positive leader among his peers.

Mookie accompanied me on a missions trip. During a worship service, he experienced a breakthrough. He began to feel conflicted inside and broke down sobbing with grief, pain, and regret. He ended up confessing that when he was younger he witnessed a murder, but did not tell anyone about it. Although this behavior was in accordance with the code of the hood ("snitches get stitches"), and the incident involved a kind of street justice, it caused him a great deal of conflict and pain. He had buried the memory for years and years, never telling anyone what he had seen. At this point of deeper commitment to Christ, the memory and pain emerged. He unburdened himself, crying on my shoulder as I hugged him. Mookie was able to release this burden, abandoning his cool persona, and ask for forgiveness. For him to be able to let his guard down to express and let go of this pain was a huge breakthrough in his growth as a Christian and as a man. Mookie became stronger in his relationship with Christ, a stronger man, and a more open and free person, who was at peace with himself and others.

Mookie's situation is not an uncommon one among his peer group. In working with boys in my community, I may find myself dealing with deep feelings of pain, grief, and loss, often culminating in violence and anger. It can happen at the drop of a hat, or the turn of a corner. There's no telling what may trigger a series of connections that will result in debilitating emotion. But there is deep-seated trauma in many youth, induced by witnessing a murder or other act of violence or physical or even verbal abuse. Unless addressed, they will never get past it to develop into stable and secure adults. Psychologists refer to it as "psychic trauma," a form of post-traumatic stress disorder (PTSD), which often manifests as "a learning disability, hyperactivity, or an attention deficit disorder."[1]

I have witnessed triggered episodes while transporting youth to and from basketball practice or games, or when away from home and neighborhood at one of our camps, many times during high-stress situations, but not always. A seemingly violent outburst is often a much-needed release of bottled-up emotion, followed by a brief moment of vulnerability. I deal with those situations by being present, listening, grieving, and mourning with them—whatever the situation requires—and offering prayer because these events are breakthroughs, times of opportunity for counsel and comfort.

Manhood Camp is part of the *Young Lions* mentoring program, during which we have adopted a custom called the Pain Fire. Its purpose is to allow participants to express their deepest feelings in a safe environment. At the Pain Fire, as mentors and mentees sit around a large campfire, the younger participants are invited to share a time in their lives when they have experienced emotional pain. Each one has been given a stick. At first, they are slow to respond, but the campfire setting in the woods at night promotes an atmosphere conducive to sharing. Invariably when one starts, the others follow along pretty quickly. Sharing stories of feeling neglect, grief, fear, or anger experienced from the hands of family, friends, or peers or from just living in the hood, they throw the stick into the fire. After each story, the group recites a prayer mantra, "Lord, hear our prayer." At the Pain Fire, we don't try to fix problems. The goal is simply to get the campers to open up about their feelings and talk. Throwing the stick into the fire symbolizes giving our pain to God, whom they can trust to take care of us.

One time, a mentor shared about his relationship with his father, who had left his family when he was young. This man was about to be married and was working through some implications of starting a family. As soon as he was done, the participants peppered him with questions about how he felt about his dad. Ninety percent of them had no fathers at home. One of the questions that struck me the most was, "Even though you are angry with your father, do you still love him?" Through sharing his pain and feeling, this mentor helped the boys to work through some of their own feelings about their absent fathers. Interactions like these provide positive interpersonal relationships and opportunities for younger participants to open up and identify and share their feelings. In this way, we can circumvent the culture of isolation among young men in urban neighborhoods. As Black men, we need to help each other and support each other, and God is our ever-present source of strength.

HOME

Another critical cultural tension that must be addressed is that of the home. The tension surrounding the concept of home may best be described through a syndicated (1989–1995) comic strip called *Outland*, created by Berkeley Breathed, an American cartoonist and creator of children's books who won the Pulitzer Prize for Editorial Cartooning in 1987. The story begins with a little African American girl named Ronald-Ann Smith, who lived in a harsh environment. Her neighborhood was plagued by gang violence, drug dealing, and drug abuse. There are no attentive, caring adults in her world. Finding such an existence too difficult to cope with, she escapes to an imaginary place called Outland, the entrance to which is gained through a magical door at the end of the alley behind the projects where she lives. Outland is a bright and beautiful place, populated with strange and wonderful creatures who care about Ronald-Ann and are attentive to her.

The whole story is presented as an urban take on the Dorothy and the *Wizard of Oz* tale. However, upon being compared to Dorothy, Ronald-Ann comments about the girl who was whisked away to a place of magic and adventure with wonderful friends but while there could think only of how to get back home: "I never bought that part." In the last frame of the strip, one of Outland's residents states: "Home: frequently overrated."[2]

While the idealized image of home is one of a secure place with caring adults where one's needs are consistently met, for many children in the inner city, this is not the case. It is rather a place of dysfunctional relationships, overwhelming stress, and a continuous struggle to survive; a place rife with experiences of pain, suffering, grief, and neglect. Home is a place from which some children, even as they all love their parents and siblings, may need respite in the form of enrichment programs at church, at school, or in the community, which engender positive relationships. This creates a false dichotomy of extreme loyalty to home and family, which exists alongside the cognizance of their often destructive nature. Dysfunction, stress, and want become a normal state of being; feelings of stability become alien to them. A critical tension necessary in any effort by the urban youth worker to minister to children and youth is to be aware of this dynamic, but to also respect the home and parental authority.

A youth worker may show respect and practice common courtesy by checking in with the parent whenever he or she visits the child or provides an outing. No matter how many fun or meaningful activities or experiences the mentor or youth worker may share with that child, that child still must return home. Many times a youth worker is trapped between looking out for the welfare of the child and attempting to support the family infrastructure. In extreme cases it may be the youth worker who must report cases of neglect or abuse to the proper authorities. Regardless of the circumstances at that home, no matter the youth worker's personal experience of home or his or her biases, simple human contact and courtesy go a long way toward building authentic and redemptive relationships with the family and the child. Time taken to connect with the parent of a child is time well invested for ministry. For good or bad, the home environment is the primary factor in shaping a child's outcome.

Family and home are tremendous allies in discipleship efforts. What does it mean to be a Christian in the context of the culture of a home that is antithetical to that ideal?

Being a Christian *is* countercultural, even in a mainstream society that calls itself Christian and that promotes certain ideals of home and family. But for a young Black male, being a disciple of Christ can be countercultural within his own family. We had one young teen, a streetwise kid who became a Christian and got involved in our mentoring group, sports ministry, and Bible study. He took flak from his mother regularly. She resented the fact that he wasn't behaving like other boys in the community: fighting, getting in trouble, chasing girls, and so on. She was threatened by the fact that he spent so much time involved in church activities. He'd changed his life in significant ways and had broken from examples of dysfunctional relationships and chemical abuse set by his parents and older siblings. This breaking of the cycle apparently enraged his mother. She was more upset that he had become a Christian than if he had joined a gang or gotten a girl pregnant or was dealing drugs.

Once, when I called his home, his mother angrily told me what she thought of me, chewing me out for fifteen minutes! She told me I wasn't in charge at her house, that I wasn't the kids' father, and not to call her house anymore. While I saw myself as a father figure in the absence of a positive man in this boy's life, it became difficult to continue ministering to him because my access to him was restricted after that. However, he kept coming to basketball practice and church. Though the mother would not talk to me, she hadn't forbidden him to play sports or attend Bible study. I was actually friends with this mom, and this was the third child of hers I had "adopted" with her blessing. I understood that she was concerned for her son and trying to protect him in the only way she knew how, maybe even feeling insecure as a parent. She was certainly overwhelmed with the responsibilities of being the single parent of many children. I did not return her anger but kept her in prayer. Not long afterward she called and apologized for her behavior, telling me that she was pleased to have me working with her son.

Following Christ puts some youth at odds with the behaviors and expectations of their family. A dysfunctional home context encourages children and youth to practice dishonesty, deceit, and even violence in order to attain what the individual needs or wants, in the belief that the child needs these skills to survive. Distrust of authority figures, using violence to resolve conflict, the manipulation of the system and people to gain what one needs or wants are moral standards for many among the poor. These values are antithetical to what it means to follow Christ.

To be a disciple of Christ means that the body of Christ becomes your family; it could be a church, Christian peers, or a relationship with a youth worker or pastor. For our kids it is often the basketball team. New Christians must align their primary loyalty to the family of God. For teens already walking a tightrope between loyalty to peers and birth family, the whole issue of the primacy of relationship with Christ compared to that with family is a delicate one. I never ask kids to abandon their family, but I do challenge them to put Christ first. In Bible study, when I utilize Matthew 10:37—"Those who love father or mother more than me aren't worthy of me"—as a discussion point for this issue, I can see the shock in their eyes. For most people, family is one's first loyalty, but for Black youth, to put anything before your family is blasphemous. In spite of the complexity of inner-city life and the stresses that go with it, association with family is the highest bond.

Back in the day, in the hood and in Black communities in general, you didn't let anyone say anything negative about your mom. Mom represented the most stable and dependable force in a child's life. If anyone said anything derogatory about your mom, you were obligated to fight and defend her honor. If you didn't, you lost all respect among your peers, and if it got home that you didn't fight, you got a whuppin'. It didn't matter if the person who insulted your mom was twice as big as you. It didn't matter if you lost the fight. You just didn't let people insult your mom. It's hard to describe the visceral response such an insult would evoke in Black boys. It's like letting loose the floodgates of anger and grief and sorrow. Many a Goliath has fallen to a little David for talking about his mom.

Nowadays, that is not the case. Drug addiction, particularly to crack-cocaine, has taken its toll on some Black families in urban communities. First, it was the rampant heroin addiction in the 1960s, which helped spawn the increase of single, female-headed families in urban areas through the decimation of Black men; then in the 1980s, the crack epidemic began wreaking havoc in urban communities and destroying families, reaching even some Black mothers. This highly and quickly addictive substance created mothers who, because of the effect crack has on the brain, could not connect with their babies and women who would do anything to get the quick and intense high. Because the mother is often the lynchpin in Black households, this addiction ultimately resulted in the breakdown of the family. For some communities, the status of the mother as the primary figure in the Black family suffered. This esteem is now often reserved for the matriarch of the family—grandma—often known as "Madear" or "Big Mama." The highest oath some may express among themselves is on the life of their grandmother: "I'm telling the truth. I put that on my grandma!"

In the Bible, Jesus tells a rich young man that if he wants to be a disciple, he must sell everything he owns and give the money to the poor. After the man walks away and Jesus describes how difficult it is to enter the kingdom of God, Peter exclaims, "We've left everything and followed you." Jesus promises that anyone who leaves house, siblings, parents, or property for Christ (all the things that make for abundant life on earth) will receive them back better than can be imagined (it wouldn't be easy); in addition, they will receive eternal life (Mark 10:28-30). In Matthew 8:18-22, Jesus tells a man that he should let nothing come before following him, including the burying of his father, that is, even family. Christ has to be first. God doesn't take second place to anyone or anything. Black males in the hood understand about loyalty. To be disciples of Christ, they must surrender their families to Christ, along with every other part of their lives. But what they surrender, Jesus takes, restores, and multiplies.

RELATIONSHIPS

The struggle of life in the inner city also puts undue stress upon individual relationships, those within as well as those surrounding the family context. Relationships become a casualty of the struggle to just get by every day, becoming competitive, vindictive, and petty. This can happen in human relationships in general, but the confluence of poverty, crime, and violence often found in urban communities bodes ill for sustaining meaningful relationships in any form. In these communities, persons rarely trust anyone enough to call them friend. The dynamics of survival engenders a basic distrust of institutions, people, and one another. The stresses faced can be overwhelming and take a drastic toll on familial relationships.

The primary relationship for all children is mom, even for those at-risk. For too many African American males, this relationship is fraught with unrequited love and need. The boy loves his mother, and the mother loves the child—but that's not enough. The boy needs his mother; her very presence is sustenance, but she is often not able to be there for the child the way she desires to be. A case in point: Jamaal, a fifth-grade mentee on my basketball team, had been missing school for a week, yet he was calling me to pick him up for basketball practices and games. When I called his mom to find out why he wasn't at school, she told me she thought he had been going to school. She explained that she had to leave home every morning to go to work before the school bus came, and that he was supposed to get on the bus and go to school. She was grateful when I offered to get involved and make sure the boy got on the bus to go to school.

Single mothers are often working low-paying jobs, sometimes more than one, that barely bring in the income needed to meet basic needs for food, shelter, and clothing. They are consumed with the responsibility for the care and nurture of children and for ordering their lives.

In Minneapolis, close to 60 percent of poor families "over North" are headed by single moms. Handicapped economically due to lack of education, opportunity, and sustainable jobs, they typically live from crisis to crisis—from negotiating welfare programs, to the educational system, to the courts without emotional or any kind of support from a partner. Nurturing may come second, third, or fourth in the list of things their children need, after housing, food, or medical care. Mother is too overwhelmed and stressed to give Jamaal all the nurture and attention he craves and deserves.

Jamaal often has no relationship with his father. If he knows his father, the man is not at home. He is in jail or residing on the other side of town or in another city living a separate life, sometimes with another family. If father is at home, he is often engaged in such negative and unhealthy behavior that his impact on the family is much worse than if he was absent. Additionally, parental ties with a father figure are nonexistent. Uncles, grandfathers, or even grandmothers may pick up the slack of parental guidance, but for the most part, the concept of father as a guide and model of manhood is nowhere on the grid. Other men in Jamaal's life are men out in the street or possibly boyfriends of his mother, the worst-case scenario being a revolving door of men coming in and out without attachment because they never stay long enough, but each leaving behind a negative imprint.

It is not uncommon for families like a Jamaal's to have a number of children, each with different fathers. Such sibling bonds are often weak and relationships are ones of convenience. Siblings often feel as if they have to compete with each other for their mother's affection. Perhaps some of the siblings' fathers are more involved than others, and this sets up a competitive dynamic and feelings of jealousy among them. In the same house, one sibling gets shoes and clothing from an absent father while brother and sister go without. The ideal of family unity is substituted with envy, competition, and strife. In fact, every relationship becomes some form of competition, an extension of the struggle for survival and to have one's emotional needs meet.

Relational bonds made outside of the family unit are often the strongest, for good or ill. There is a natural camaraderie with boys in the peer group who face the same issues in their homes. This is often what drives them to be involved with gangs. They find a solidarity and sense of community and belonging that they do not experience at home: hurting children bonding together to form an allegiance of sorts against the world. And yet, relationships with children and adults alike are fraught with mistrust and deceit. Institutional relationships, such as with school teachers or employers, which will have an overwhelming impact on Jamaal as he matures, are tremendously difficult as a result of deep-seated distrust of authority.

Relationships are simply not a viable currency in street life. Jamaal does not have any friends, anyone that he trusts and depends on, only associates, people of casual acquaintance. He has learned early that trust is betrayed, even by those he is supposed to be able to depend on, and betrayal hurts. It's obvious that he is not valuable to anyone else, so he is not valuable to himself. Instead of gaining a sense of self-worth, positive self-image, and strong self-esteem from his family unit, he has developed a skewed image of himself. He does not regard himself as valuable, worthy of love, as special or unique in any way. Having little or no esteem, he does not have esteem for others.

Jamaal carries all this baggage into relationships with girls. The only male and female relationships he's witnessed have been characterized by selfishness, abuse, lack of commitment, and stress. He's been taught by example that women are objects to be dominated and abused for satisfying sexual or material needs. Children may be an unfortunate consequence of carelessness, but at any rate they are the woman's responsibility. The relationships he has seen are based on distrust, control, and abuse. Jamaal does not know how to love or be loved. For someone to break through this pattern of distrust and build a genuine and authentic relationship with a young person in this setting takes time and hard work.

What does it mean to be a Christian in an environment of such unhealthy relationships? One family I worked with was consumed with fractured and dysfunctional relationships like those I just described. There seemed no way for this family to break the cycle of substance abuse, gang involvement, and neglected children. When I made pastoral visits, the parents would be sitting in the living room stoned, with evidence of drug use lying right out in front of me. I kept up my involvement with the children, confronting their parents about their self-destructive behavior, but the family continued to spiral ever downward.

At that time my wife was pregnant and on bed rest with our first child and needed me at home. This family was constantly in crisis and was calling on me frequently to help them. I referred them to a program that specialized in helping people overcome their chemical addictions. I felt like I had abandoned them and cast them off to the street—but a miracle happened. They hit bottom, but they did not fall apart. Part of the new treatment program was attending church and discipleship. They ceased using drugs and changed their lifestyle. The father, who was a major gang figure, cut off all associations with his gang. In a short time, they were living drug-free and setting good examples for their kids in every aspect of family life.

I continued working with the children and I could see that things had changed. I could see through my continued visits that family life had become much different. The children continued to struggle with the legacy of generations of abuse and neglect, but I could tell by their demeanor that they were happy and cared for at home. This was a different family, more cohesive, more positive and more supportive of one another. Both mom and dad found jobs, the family attended church together, and the kids' emotional and physical needs were attended to. They have experienced substantive change and it's because of Christ in their lives.

THE OPPOSITE SEX

It is peculiar how the absence of fathers can affect male-female relationships in growing males. On a South African game preserve, "delinquent" young male elephants were attacking endangered rhinoceroses, bullying and killing them. Research into the problem revealed that the issues stemmed from the removal of all the mature male elephants from the herd for breeding and relocation. "The program created a whole generation of traumatized orphans thrown together without any adults to teach them how to behave."[3] The "orphans," upon becoming teenagers, began to run rampant on the preserve, targeting rhinos and often sexually assaulting them. The solution was simple enough: undo what they had done in disturbing the development of the young elephants by reintroducing mature male elephants into the herd. The mentoring by the older males had the desired effect on the younger males; the violent behavior ceased. What is true in the animal kingdom is true for human beings. Boys need fathers or, failing that, other positive role models to step in the gap and help them figure out what it means to be a man.

Warped relationships with the opposite sex are a product of low self-esteem and the persona of coolness cultivated by the Jamaals of the world. While being respected is of the utmost importance to them, they have a hard time bestowing respect toward others, particularly women. The attitude of the average young man toward women may be seen in popular rap and hip hop songs. Women are seen as sexual objects or things, material aspects of the trappings of success. In music videos, women are clad in ways that emphasize their sexuality; they gyrate their bodies to the beat. They are not seen as equals or deserving of respect or even polite consideration. On the contrary, in videos and music lyrics, women are referred to as a b------ and *ho*.

Inner-city boys who revere and emulate these artists take on these values and impose them on the women in their lives. These are, of course, unrealistic portrayals of women, and fallacious and destructive attitudes to adhere to, but they are common. Young women and girls will often debase themselves in order to fulfill male fantasies. Today some hip hop women artists are just as misogynistic as males, adopting derogatory terms for themselves. The problem is often exacerbated by the witness of abusive behavior toward women and girls in the home and in the hood. The issues between Black men and Black women are deeply complex and historically ingrained, affecting the quality of Black family life. It takes a Herculean amount of work and influence to unlearn negative attitudes toward the opposite sex and to begin to learn appropriate new ones. Mentors and mentees alike are working against centuries of ingrained self-destructive behavior and attitudes going back to slave days.

Urban culture as a whole has had a devastating effect on Black boys' relationship with the opposite sex. Black boys aspire to be "playas" (players), another one of those negative role models perpetuated in hip hop music, the quintessential self-image of the young urban Black male. A playa is one who has multiple women at his beck and call, treats them disdainfully, and uses them for sex. All the guys think it is the height of coolness to be a playa. Ironically, the whole concept of being a playa was forced on their ancestors by slaveholders. Enslaved men were often forced to copulate with many partners in order to increase the slave stock of their owners. As a result, the male slave was surrounded on a plantation by children who were likely his, but he was not allowed to be a father to any of them. It is vital that boys be disabused of such a notion of "playa" if they are to have any hope of a fulfilling life. The debilitating effect of this and other self-destructive attitudes has taken a horrendous toll on the family unit.

Relationships with the opposite sex take on an unhealthy and distorted aspect. Sex is casual, with vastly different consequences and import for males and females. For boys, it is a quick way to get street cred; for girls, it is a means to gain acceptance and belonging through having children. For males, it contributes to their self-esteem for obvious reasons, boosting their macho images and cool personas. For females, getting pregnant and bearing children brings standing in the family, home, or community, as well as providing an innocent, fresh source of love and dependence. Many positive male and female relationships exist in urban communities like mine, but the abusive behavior I have been describing is definitely the default attitude among most young Black males. Relationships between men and women vary from faithful unions between two people, albeit without the traditional social sanctions of marriage, to associations of convenience, or, at worst, abuse and codependence.

Even the once-revered mother figure can potentially be reviled as boys mature and move on from their influence. Growing up in a household where the mother is abused or taken advantage of by men, teens learn that it is OK for men to revile or disrespect women, even to the point of physical abuse. They experience conflicted feelings about motherhood because they often see their mothers debased by a man at home, by absentee fathers and boyfriends. Boys revere and respect their mom, but they will revile and disrespect other women. They learn that if a woman disrespects a man or does him wrong, the man has a right—no, an obligation—to set her straight, even if it requires the use of physical force. Young people we work with have been present when my wife and I have an argument or strong disagreement; they are surprised when it doesn't degenerate into violence.

As part of my influence, I demonstrate and teach early and vigorously that young men are not to speak disrespectfully about women and that it is wrong for a man to do so. Don't do it around me! This flies in the face of everything most of them have seen and heard about male and female relationships. However, the work of Christ in their lives will redeem relationships corrupted by their dysfunctional environments. When they begin to learn who they are in Christ and build accurate self-images, their attitudes, suppositions, and relationships with the opposite sex can and do change.

CONCLUSION

In James 1:27 (NRSV), the writer admonishes the Church to practice true and pure religion that is defined by taking care of widows (women without husbands) and orphans (children without fathers) and remaining unstained by the world. It is the call for all believers to live a life for Christ and not be conformed to this world (Romans 12:2). Christians must live in this world, but we must not become part of it. Christian youth in urban communities have the same mandate; they may live in the hood, but must not belong to it.

Despite the unique challenges of environment and culture, they can find a way to live out the Christian call. They can choose another path, realizing that life in Christ enables all to rise above the context of their culture and environment to live lives pleasing to God. This does not mean that they must conform to the mainstream culture, which is how some interpret Christianity; rather there is a higher culture of Christ in the kingdom of God to which we all must aspire.

We all must work to be unstained by our sinful, worldly environment until Jesus returns to take us all home. Young people may accomplish this by disassociating themselves from their environment and choosing positive, self-affirming pursuits and associations. They don't have to buy into the negativity and hopelessness their environment may engender. All Christians, no matter the context, require God's power to do this. For the Christian, the Holy Spirit works within to make all things, including one's context and environment, new. Second Corinthians 5:17 tells us: "So then, if anyone is in Christ, that person is part of the new creation. The old things have gone away, and . . . new things have arrived!"

Knowing Jesus and who you are in Christ changes the stress-laden dynamics of peers, home, and relationships. Bringing God to the situation is a soothing balm for distrust and abuse. When a person is in Christ, everything can be viewed from a different perspective and acted upon from enlightened motivations—everything is new. A person is not bound to the dehumanizing effects of institutional racism or the effects of poverty. The youth worker or pastor is an agent of Christ, providing a new experience of what relationship should be, which then becomes a blueprint for all others in life. An evolving friendship with Jesus helps youth to learn about trust, openness, and faithfulness. They may begin anew building the basic patterns for a life that is self-affirming and fulfilling, based on a fundamental love and respect for self and fulfilling, authentic relationships with others.

CHAPTER FIVE

JUST WANNA
BE HAPPY

Several years ago I was working with someone who was and is very dear to my heart. I first met Rashawn during lunch in the cafeteria at the high school. He was with his friends and when we were introduced, I felt like God was drawing me to him. We became attached immediately. I'd get him from school or his house and we'd hang out together playing basketball at the park or going to get something to eat and doing Bible study with other kids in my small group. We were tight. As tight as a person could be with Rashawn. He lived with his dad, but never felt like his dad cared about him. To Rashawn his dad was stern, mean, and borderline abusive. Rashawn never felt accepted for who he was. He came with me on a lot of the stress-reducing trips that my church would sponsor: camping, biking, rock climbing, hiking. It was during one of these that he gave his life to Christ.

Rashawn was a popular kid. He was good-looking and had a great personality. Girls liked him and he was bright. But there was something off about Rashawn. He was never satisfied with what he had, he always wanted more. He was never content or at peace. Rashawn was always trying to "get over." He was the master of doing just enough to get by. He was manipulative, secretive, and evasive. He always had his secrets, and he was always working the angles to see what he could get, or what he could get away with. He would smile in your face and plot your betrayal in his mind if it helped him get what he wanted. But the question was, What did he want? I don't think he knew. He always wanted something more or better than what he had. The grass was always greener on the other side of the fence. What he had or what he could do never satisfied him. If he had a steady girlfriend, he would ruin the relationship by running around with other girls. If he had a good job, he would lose it by showing up to work late or being lazy and indifferent in his tasks. At school he was capable of getting As but he would slide by with Cs. He was never in trouble over his behavior, but his behavior would always be right on the edge. He was a manipulator, a player, a con man.

One day, during group Bible study, he scrawled profane graffiti on the wall of my apartment. I didn't discover it until the next day, and when I found it, I was incensed that he had vandalized my home like that. I felt he had no respect for our relationship. I found him at school that day and confronted him. At first, he wouldn't admit that he had done it. He kept denying it and saying he didn't know how it got there. I was really angry and over the next several times we met we were hammering out this issue. Finally he said, "What's the big deal? Why do you care so much?" He couldn't understand why I was upset and disappointed in him. I said, "Rashawn, it's not the wall that makes me angry. It's the fact that you care so little about our relationship that you would do something like that and not own up to it." He realized that I wasn't going to let it go. He admitted he did it and apologized.

I think it would've been easier for him if I had gotten angry and never hung out with him again. He probably wondered why that didn't happen. I wouldn't let it go. I forced him to deal with it and with me. He was used to people getting angry and then leaving him. Like everything else to Rashawn, relationships were just fodder for his amusement and tools to manipulate people to get what he wanted out of them. It surprised him that ours meant so much to me. Rashawn had a lot going for him compared to his peers: looks, personality, smarts.

But it was never enough. He was always looking for something more. Personal satisfaction and happiness escaped him. He was always driven to sabotage what he had in the hopes of finding something better. Never satisfied, never fulfilled, Rashawn didn't know how to be happy. He was never satisfied with anything, because he wasn't satisfied with himself.

THE ABSENCE OF HOPE

Happiness, satisfaction, and peace are what every person desires. The US Constitution protects each citizen's life and liberty, and the Declaration of Independence describes the "pursuit of happiness" as an inalienable right. But many Black males growing up in the inner city feel left out of this contract. "How can I be happy," they ask, "when everything around me points to despair and hopelessness?" The issue of being happy refers to personal satisfaction, contentment, and fulfillment in life. Contentment is to be happy and satisfied, to be at peace with one's self and one's circumstances. The pursuit of happiness is about opportunity, having the opportunity to gain all of the above. The emotional state of many at-risk Black youth every day is not one of contentment or even the ability or opportunity to pursue contentment, but of strife, a struggle to simply get through the day, or to get over. To *get over* means to get what you need in life for that day, for that moment, by any means necessary. To survive in the context of inner-city America, one must know how to get over. One doesn't plan for the future; a person works to get what is needed for that moment, then worries about the next moment, never satisfied because of always looking for the next needed thing. The future doesn't matter, only the present moment.

Rashawn was obsessed with getting over. That's all that was important to him. Relationships with family or friends didn't matter, nor did school or work. These were all tools to be manipulated to help him get over, to get what he could when he could get it. He was only interested in what he could get for himself for that moment. It was difficult to establish a relationship with him. I knew him for many years, but I don't know that we ever did establish a genuine relationship. I know I was closer to him than any other adult in his life. He wanted to be happy, but he didn't know how. He thought he could gain happiness at the expense of others, but he was never at peace. He was always trying to get more,

> # The despair of hopelessness results in violence and disregard for life, society, and relationships.

and there was always the next big thing. He never expected any genuinely good thing he experienced to last. He could never relax and enjoy it because he was worried about what was next. He was suspicious of people and relationships in his life because he expected to be used and manipulated by them. He had no hope or expectation of lasting joy or peace in his life.

In order for youth to pursue happiness in substantive ways for long-term effect, the ability to hope must first be instilled. Hopelessness is a disease run rampant among poor families. The despair of hopelessness results in violence and disregard for life, society, and relationships. Some among the poor in Minneapolis refer to the city as "Minnehopeless." This nickname alludes not only to economic struggles but also to the social and spiritual anguish of living life on the fringe of society. Because they have no real hope for lasting and genuine peace, their attempts to find happiness are sabotaged by their own behaviors and attitudes. Every time they are on a path to wholeness, they seem to find ways to sabotage themselves. That's the way Rashawn and many young men behave.

It takes many restarts for people who have been conditioned to hopelessness to stay on a path to healing. A critical component for pursuing wholeness is simply to have someone in their corner who believes in them. This is why recovering addicts and alcoholics need sponsors. For young people, the consistent encouragement of a caring adult goes a long way to helping them stick to positive avenues of seeking affirmation and success. Although staying in relationship with Rashawn felt like repeatedly running into a brick wall, I felt like I was able to make a difference in his life.

An example of this kind of despair is the young man who came to Lisa and me for help to get a start in his life. We'd known him since he was a child. His father had never been in the picture and his mother had abandoned him at the age of seventeen. He'd appeared on our doorstep with nothing, needing shelter, food, and drink. We fed him and sheltered him for a while. We helped him find a place to stay and he found a job. I got him enrolled in a trade school and he was working on his GED. It seemed like things were moving forward, but one day after he'd left our house, we noticed he had gone in my wallet and stolen money. I was flabbergasted. Not only were we in close relationship with him, we were also literally the only people he knew who were willing and able to help him. When confronted with his theft, he made no excuses, just said he was sorry. Driven by despair, he saw his opportunity, took the money, and ran. Even when things were beginning to look up for him, he just could not believe that things were going to get better.

Young people need someone to tell them they can make it. Hope, or the lack thereof, is an issue of critical importance in empowering the poor in urban communities. Hope is a determining factor in the potential of an individual to experience a life of fulfillment or satisfaction. The hope that things will get better is a primary component in the psyche of those who successfully navigate suffering, whatever its form. Hope is a critical factor in experiencing and living a victorious Christian life. The assertion of the apostle Paul, that Christ is in you, "the hope of glory" (Colossians 1:27), is the essence of the faith and hope that enables the Christian to follow Christ daily.

Evangelical Christianity maintains that the conviction of sin leading to repentance and forgiveness is the foundation of the conversion experience. However, I have found that of no less importance in regard to the evangelism and discipleship of Black youth is to engender hope. Inner-city dwellers have no problem grasping the concept of sin. Because they are witnesses to daily struggles with unhealthy lifestyle choices, inner-city youth understand full well the biblical passage, "The heart is deceitful above all things / and beyond cure. / Who can understand it?" (Jeremiah 17:9 NIV). Urban dwellers understand repentance and receive God's grace and forgiveness of sins through the blood of Jesus because they know that they need it. One may never truly understand the healing of grace without having experienced the ravages of sin. Hopelessness, not repentance, is often a barrier to salvation and trust in God. Repentance is related to hope in that one repents of one's sin with the hope that God will forgive, and that one may indeed change ingrained sinful behavior with God's help. But hope is an alien emotion among many hurting youth. They have no hope that things will get better, that with hard work and sincere effort they will succeed at school, a job, or a relationship. They are resigned to hopelessness and simply live for the day, eking out fleeting moments of peace and satisfaction. If they cannot hope or trust in what they can see, how can they hope in what they cannot see? Hopelessness then is a barrier to faith, without which no one may approach God. But thank goodness for the gospel message, that Christ brings hope where there is no hope.

A DREAM DEFERRED

In his poem "Harlem," African American poet Langston Hughes asks what happens when dreams are curtailed and hope is denied. He wonders if the dream dries up, or festers, or sags, then concludes with the suggestive, ominous possibility: "*Or does it explode?*"[1]

It exploded in North Minneapolis in 2002 when residents and neighbors rioted after the police inadvertently shot and wounded a boy during a drug raid (and again exploded in 2020 with the police murder of George Floyd). Crowd violence and property destruction occurred in the explosive expression of anger, frustration, and hopelessness by community residents. Tensions were high from a recent shooting of a young Black man by police. The denial of justice, the denial of dreams, the denial of hope squash the human spirit, sometimes prompting communal eruptions, but most of the time the eruption stems from an individual and personal nature. Sometimes violently, sometimes in quiet acquiescence to despair and hopelessness.

This is the weight carried by many young people . . . the burden of dreams deferred, never realized, dreams never born, as the poet writes. They cannot afford to hope when the debilitating experience of disappointment looms. Broken hearts and crushed psyches are left in the wake of dashed dreams and broken promises. Educational consultant Jawanza Kunjufu alludes to this dynamic in his book *Countering the Conspiracy to Destroy Black Boys*, identifying it as the "fourth grade failure syndrome."[2] He observes that young African American boys at early ages and primary grade levels exhibit exuberance and openness in their attitudes toward life and school. However, around the fourth-grade level (age nine) they begin to harden and become more intractable by stages. It is at this stage of development that they begin to internalize negative social messages they see in society: that being Black and poor is about the lowest rung on the ladder of success to the American dream.

What is there for them to be happy about? Statistically, they have the highest rates for crime, murder, incarceration, unemployment, illiteracy, and truancy. This demographic is about as far away from the traditional American dream as a person could be. The syndrome of self-negating behavior identified by Kunjufu is occurring among Black boys at younger and younger ages. In public school systems all over the country there is great consternation among educators and parents about the increasing rate of suspensions among Black male children and the persistent achievement gap between them and their White counterparts. Black boys are getting suspended from school as early as preschool, continuing to first and second grade. What kind of behavior from these young children could possibly necessitate suspension from school? The answer: behavior that threatens the physical safety of other students or even adult teachers in the classroom.

Children are learning dysfunctional behavior at early ages and simply emulate what has been modeled for them. I've visited in homes where toddlers were running around the house ranting and raving in frightening ways, their faces contorted with anger, grief, and confusion borne out of neglect and abuse. Six-year-old boys are experiencing feelings of anger that they do not understand or know what to do with. In the North Side elementary school where I volunteer, I see six- and seven-year-old boys caught up in paroxysms of grief and rage that they cannot control and teacher and administrators are unable to assuage. This is a direct result of experiencing trauma at home or in the community. At a young age, they are beginning to see that there is no brass ring in life for them, only disillusionment, disappointment, and failure.

From young ages, the dreams of poor Black boys are crushed, similar to what Malcolm X shared in his autobiography. As a young student, when asked what he wanted to be when he grew up he replied that he wanted to be a lawyer. His White teacher shook his head and told him to be more realistic; a Black boy like him was more suited to be a carpenter or laborer of some sort. Dreams of young boys die *in utero* when they lack role models in their community of men who are living out their visions of being lawyers, doctors, teachers, and so on. Dreams of Black boys are dashed when they are held to much lower standards of performance in their classrooms and schools, and their teachers don't expect them to learn or achieve. Their dreams are crushed when they are watching their favorite show on television and when the commercials come on they see affluent White people living in big houses in suburban neighborhoods driving nice cars and they think, "That isn't me." Their dreams are restricted to the arenas of professional sports or the entertainment industry because that's where they see wealthy, significant Black people. Almost every young Black boy in the city when asked what he wants to be when he grows up will answer professional athlete or rap/hip hop artist. How can poor Black boys dream when they don't know what to dream about? How can poor Black boys dream when they have no experience or firsthand knowledge of the unlimited possibilities that are available to them? We need to teach our boys how to dream by exposing them to African American role models from various occupational fields. Going on field trips is an excellent way to expose boys to career and vocational possibilities. They need experiences that showcase their heritage as African Americans and the unique contributions of their culture to American society in the areas of science, music, technology—and yes, sports and entertainment. In the post-Obama presidency era, we can even add politics to that list.

Every year on the way to summer camp, we stop at the George Washington Carver National Monument in Diamond, Missouri. George Washington Carver was born a slave on a plantation in Missouri. At a young age, he and his mother were kidnapped by raiders, and although he was rescued, his mother was killed. His slave owners subsequently adopted and raised him as their own child. From such debilitating beginnings, he became a world-renowned scientist. His agricultural research completely changed the lives and prospects of ex-slaves and other poor people in the South by giving them a means to gain economic power. Carver was asked how he overcame such obstacles in his life. His response is mounted on a wall inside the monument: "As a child I was convinced that I could accomplish whatever I set my mind to, and what I set my mind to was exploration and learning." We must help our youth dream by telling them that they can do it! Whatever they set their minds to do is possible for them to accomplish.

UNLEARNING NEGATIVITY

In order to be happy, youth must unlearn the negativity imprinted by their environment and learn to be positive. They must unlearn

- societal messages that they do not count because they are poor and Black;
- messages that they are not to be trusted and that they are to be feared because they are Black and male;
- messages that there is no hope for the kind of life they want, so they might as well get what they can right now, because this is all they can expect;
- self-destructive behavior of violence and abuse, practiced in anger and rebellion;
- self-denigrating speech in which they put themselves and others down.

They must begin to work through the dysfunctional issues plaguing their families and personal relationships.

It is much harder to unlearn ingrained behavior than to learn new behavior. One 2002 study in Minneapolis on the status of African American men revealed staggering figures.

- Nearly half of Black men ages eighteen to thirty are arrested by police.
- Black men are twice as likely as young White men to die before they reach the age of twenty-four.
- Almost 50 percent of young Black men living in poverty in the most dangerous neighborhoods of Minneapolis are born to single mothers.
- Close to 75 percent do not graduate high school in four years.
- Close to 50 percent drop out of school.[3]

The study (African American Men Project, Hennepin County Office of Planning and Development, Minneapolis) purports that in addition to social service programs addressing these needs, African American men must be part of the answer in reversing these trends. While not excusing the effect of historic and systemic racism, or the impact of socioeconomic factors, Black men must also take responsibility. In discussing these points with participants in the *Young Lions* program, one commented: "We keep doing the same thing!" This child actually put his finger on the problem—that the behavior of dysfunctional adult Black men reflected in this study is the same as that practiced by him and his peers in school, engendering the same results, behavioral referrals, and school suspensions. The negative self-destructive behavior we learn as children becomes ingrained and repeated as we mature into adulthood. We keep doing the same thing. One young man in this study commented that many young men his age don't have a sense of hope because "they don't see how things can change."[4] We have to help our young men unlearn negativity and learn to hope.

Often this demographic is trying to achieve the goals of happiness and satisfaction in a vacuum of genuine community. They are out there in the world without the support and encouragement they need to accomplish their heart's desire or pursue their dreams. The only community these young men regularly experience is the dysfunctional family, peer group, and neighborhood. There is rarely support for achieving positive goals for education and personal development. Those who succeed in this environment are those who are able to build around themselves a network of support that provides encouragement and nurture.

For example, consider Isaiah. He was raised by a single parent, his father. His mother left the family when he was six, having become addicted to crack cocaine. His father was devoted to raising Isaiah and his two older brothers, but he had failing health. He died when Isaiah was sixteen. Isaiah's two older brothers dropped out of school and did the best they could to take care of themselves and Isaiah, but struggled with their own issues in the streets. At a young age, Isaiah began weaving a web of support for himself through relationships with caring neighbors, local churches, youth workers, and positive friends. In spite of his environment, and watching many of his peers fall to street life, Isaiah maintained a positive outlook on life and a positive self-image. He worked hard to achieve milestones, like becoming the first in his family to graduate from high school. He is now a technical college graduate and makes a good living working at his trade, as well as raising a family. Isaiah made it against all odds, demonstrating an unexpected resiliency. His network was composed of people he sought out (friends, neighbors, pastors, and teachers from various sources and agencies) and from whom he received encouragement and support in substantive ways.

How do you build community with at-risk, estranged youth? In the case with Isaiah, community consisted of genuine relationships built over a significant period of time. Relationships of trust and respect cannot develop overnight. Community meets a deeply felt need in people to belong. The problem is, Black youth are handicapped in terms of going out and having that need met. Fragmented and warped relationships, not genuine and authentic ones, are the norm for many estranged youth. Many have never had such relationships modeled for them or have never experienced such models firsthand themselves.

CONCLUSION

In order to be happy and have a chance at a fulfilling and satisfying life young Black males must nurture and cultivate hope. They can do this by putting hope and trust in the one thing that will not let them down: Christ. If they can hope, then they can dream. They can dream and imagine the kind of life they want for themselves. They can envision positive and affirming relationships, lifestyles, and career choices. If they can dream and see themselves in a different light, then they will be motivated to build networks of support and community around themselves. This network may be a mix of different people who have shown interest in the young man, but they will have one thing in common: concern for his welfare. Agencies and people of goodwill shouldn't be in competition with one another—they can work together to help each young person who comes into their sphere of influence. Eternal spiritual community and fellowship with God may only be facilitated through the body of Christ. Being spiritual beings and having a spiritual heritage, at-risk Black youth respond positively to supportive relationships within the Christian community. Above all, the young man must cultivate his own relationship with God through Christ. A relationship with God through Christ is something our youth can count on. God promises young Black men: "*I will never leave you or abandon you*" (Hebrews 13:5). Being in Christ is the only way young Black men will find fulfillment and be content, living and enjoying a sense of identity and belonging.

CHAPTER SIX

"I WANT TO GET PAID!"

BRYAN

Bryan lives in our community; I've known him since he was a teenager. I've watched him grow up, overcoming the struggles of inner-city life to become a man who works hard to accomplish his goals. He has a home, family, good job, and good standing in the community. I have a lot of respect for what he has done. Because of how he grew up, Bryan has always been driven to acquire certain material symbols of success. Family and home are very important to Bryan. His father left his family when Bryan was a teenager. They discovered that he actually had a whole other family with a different set of wife and kids. When this happened it was like the rug of life was pulled from beneath the feet of Bryan, his mother, and all of his siblings. So Bryan was always very focused on accomplishing certain things in life, to prove to himself and others that he is not like his father.

Bryan found Christ through involvement with our church youth group as a teenager and is today living a productive and fulfilling life. Bryan and I had a mentoring relationship most of his life. I was his youth worker when he was a teenager and his pastor as an adult. Despite his home and neighborhood environment, Bryan was able to stay out of trouble on the streets while he was growing up. He never yielded to the temptation to do drugs or join gangs, and he never had a child out of wedlock. He received affirmation from church and his Christian community for his positive behavior and choices, but many times he chafed at how worse-behaved kids got more attention than he did.

Bryan would always come to me for advice when he had a decision with life-changing implications, but he rarely followed it. Bryan always wanted what he wanted, and he wanted it now. He was never open to the suggestion, "Wait a little while and see how things turn out." When he became a young adult, Bryan had a great need to prove that he was a good man. To him the way to prove that was to succeed as a man in two areas that his father failed: as a husband and as a father. Bryan wanted to be somehow vindicated of the legacy of being his father's son. He wanted to be noticed by others for being someone important, meaning "You're not like your father."

Bryan wanted to be affirmed as a good man: husband to one wife, good father to his children, provider, and so on. All worthwhile goals and positive motivations! But the pitfall for Bryan was that things never happened quickly enough, or big enough. He went to college but the accolades and affirmation he sought were not forthcoming, so he quit. He got a good job that paid a fair wage, but it wasn't enough money. Nor did it give him the acclaim he sought; so, looking for something better, perhaps with more prestige, he quit. He met a girl he wanted to marry, but instead of waiting until he was financially secure, he jumped right into it. As a result he has struggled to care for his large family. He aborted many a solid plan that would yield great personal satisfaction had he given it more time, but he couldn't wait. His need for vindication and validation was immediate. Because of his need to see things happen quickly, he was left without many options for him to ease financial and social burdens. Ironically, he now found himself in a set of circumstances similar to those of his father when his father left his family.

But Bryan is a different man than his father. He takes care of his family, providing for them and the extended family as well. Having grown up in a depressed urban neighborhood, the fact that he is not addicted to drugs, in jail, or dead and is home raising wonderful children with his wife is worthy of note and affirmation. Bryan is a success because he has broken the cycle of intergenerational poverty in his family. Raised by his mom alone, he worked hard to give his children a different life. He has elevated their prospects and destinies by giving them a hopeful outlook for the future. Statistically, he is way ahead of the curve. When he was young I often asked Bryan, "What do you want out of life? What are you trying to achieve?" His response was always, "Man, I just want to get paid!"

"GETTING PAID"

You can find others like Bryan in depressed urban neighborhoods. They want what they want, and they want it now. Issues of vindication, affirmation, and satisfaction are of primary importance to them. They often encompass these yearnings in the phrase, "getting paid!" Rather than being only about monetary gain, getting paid is an issue of needing affirmation and validation, a factor that must be carefully considered when discipling Black males in the city. Often this need is couched in terms of finances and acquisitions, but money and possessions are not really the core issues. The core issues have to do with personal validation: to be valued, recognized, and affirmed for one's unique gifts, abilities, and personality. Getting paid is a metaphor for social estimation or acceptance. This is why young boys say, "When I grow up I want to get paid!" The marks of living a life of personal satisfaction in American society are painfully obvious to them—the acquisition of money, wealth, and material things. So yeah, they want the material things that the term "getting paid" so obviously means. They want to have the nice house, the nice car, and so on. Many times, it seems like these things are the privilege only of the White and affluent. In the media, it seems like the only way Black people acquire nice houses and cars is if they are professional athletes or hip hop artists. But if you are Black and poor, you don't receive positive recognition and social affirmation. Even if you are trying to make your way up the ladder of success in the mainstream, you are regarded with suspicion and as being inferior. Negative stereotypes are attached, and therefore you feel a need for vindication. Being Black and poor is to be on the bottom of the heap in American society—about as far away as you can get from getting paid.

To get paid, to be valued, appreciated, and respected for who you are—this is the goal of every red-blooded, self-respecting, ghetto male child. Whether harboring dreams of winning a million-dollar payoff on the lottery or seeing visions of making it big in professional sports, these kids want to get paid. They want to be a person of significance, value, and importance. After a while, they look around their environment, seeing dishonest and unscrupulous people taking advantage of others to get ahead, and begin to see a pattern emerge. They also observe the broader mainstream society and detect the same cutthroat and unscrupulous behavior in business and politics, and they discern the message of worldly success: "Look out for number one!" Capitalism and free enterprise are not kind to the "least of these" in American society. Otherwise the 1 percent of the US population that controls 30.4 percent of the country's household wealth would share those resources to work toward eliminating poverty and hunger. But nobody shares power, instead they hoard it. Money and wealth equals power, respect, and control. For those who are powerless in our society, particularly Black youth, these factors hold an often irresistible allure, like an elusive brass ring.

The attitude of many young men toward the inequities of society is that he will do whatever he needs to do to get what he needs for that moment. There is no thought given to future benefit or gain. So many do not want to wait to get the recognition or respect they feel they deserve. It is the rare young man in the inner city who sees hard work at school, discipline in habits, and self-control in personal behavior as the path to long-term success. However, we cannot fault them too severely because few people in mainstream society are trying to do it the hard way either, working diligently to gain success. Our society is characterized by immediate gratification and conspicuous consumption. Everyone wants to get rich quick. We all want what we want and we want it now; this has become the American way.

QUICK-FIX AFFIRMATION
VS. STRONG WORK ETHIC

Young people in depressed urban communities want what they feel is coming to them. And most of them don't expect to work too hard for it to happen; they feel they deserve it, that they've got it coming to them. Many grow up in this context angry and bitter at the world, and feeling the world is obligated to them. The concept of delayed self-gratification is foreign. This is due to being raised in families who do not model this concept, in an environment that does not appreciate this concept, and living in a society in which the rich and powerful circumvent this ideal.

However, in order to derive true satisfaction in career, education, and family, delayed self-gratification is a critical component. Young people often abort the healthy development of these goals, seeking a quick fix for money, relationships, or respect. The irony is that the quick fix is always short-lived and insubstantial. The quick fix for money or financial needs may take various forms from "get rich quick" schemes to illegal and dishonest activity such as doing crime or selling drugs. It's not enough to have earning money or living comfortably as a core value or long-term goal; it has to be immediate. In my community, I've observed that for those suffering from this particular illusion, it has to be NOW! Their ideas usually make a certain amount of sense, but the execution and end results are never what are expected. There's too much work involved. Being a professional athlete is a valid dream, but first you must finish grade school, go to high school and make good grades, and then go to college. You must begin playing sports at a young age and stay with it for many years. "Man, you got me twisted!" is the reply. Many youth don't think they should have to work hard at school or at a job to get the things they want, the things they think they deserve in life. They want to get paid now.

Evidence of quick fixes in human relationships abound in urban life. Relationships between boys and girls coming of age are entwined with sexual expectations and imperatives. Sex is casually accepted by Black teens as a part of their culture. Although teen birth rates have significantly declined in recent years, young Black girls continue to be at higher risk for teen pregnancies than their White counterparts. The birth rate of Black teens is more than twice as high as the birth rate of White teens. Underlying issues or felt needs leading to high rates of teen pregnancy may be traced to the need for love, familial connection, and physical intimacy. When it comes to sex, young boys are apt to become sexually active as soon as the opportunity presents itself because it's what's expected of them, rather than waiting for the fruition of a meaningful mature relationship with someone. Sex is just a thing guys do, and women become sexual objects. For youth, sex can be a quick fix to the affirmation and notoriety of having a child before they are capable of providing the nurture and support babies need. Young people want the affirmation of maturity and adulthood now, instead of waiting for the traditional biological and social processes.

Quick fixes for gaining respect among peers for Black males may include self-destructive behavior such as committing a crime, joining a gang, or even, in the worst-case scenario, committing a violent act. For many youth, the short path to feeling successful is acquiring the trappings of success, by any means necessary. The theft of shoes, cell phones, and the like is motivated by the feeling that this is what I need to be successful or popular, to be affirmed. There are youth whose lives were forfeited and development into adulthood aborted because of desperate attempts to gain respect by participating in violent acts and criminal schemes. Long-term avenues to gaining respect such as education, hard work, stable living, and cultivation of strong moral character hold no interest among those who are desperate to feel like they are important now. Tragically, the recognition and respect they may attain from their peers in the street from negative behavior are short-lived, cut off by prison time or death. Quick fixes by nature are just that, quick, temporary solutions that have no lasting value. Quick fixes in relation to having a good, stable life is a non sequitur; it does not follow. Emotional health, financial security, and even personal satisfaction in life come after years of seasoning by life's experiences. Generations of children miss out on their childhood pursuing quick fixes for affirmation. The benefit—even the blessing—is the journey, the time spent maturing as an individual, that is the whole point of growing up.

Many youth in the city have a "one track" attitude toward work, making it hard for them to keep a job. They will get a job to replenish their wardrobe or acquire some material possession or if they're tired of not having money in their pockets. They work for immediate, material gain and it is hard for them to see long-term goals met through hard work now. They work for a while, then quit when they got bored, or when they have enough money to get those shoes, or whatever. Those who have jobs rarely seem to be concerned with advancement or improving their situation. They are ready to quit the first time someone asks them to clean a bathroom or take out the garbage, seeing these tasks as being beneath them. They are not willing to stay on the job and work until they gain seniority and no longer have to do those tasks. One of our parishioners who grew up with us is a licensed skilled laborer. He tells me that many young Black men who come to his workplace are unable to stay on the job and work themselves into a position of stability and good wages because of the simple fact that they cannot get out of bed and show up for work on time. For many Black teenagers in my community, jobs and work are seen through the quick-fix mentality as a quick and temporary means to an end, not a long-term habit or life value, much less an end in itself for developing character. When I was given a chore as a child, my mom or dad came to inspect it. It had better be done right, or I'd have to do the whole thing over again. For me, the work ethic that I learned from my parents giving me chores has helped me succeed in my life goals, whether career, family, or personal growth. This is what all kids need, and not having it is particularly disabling for young Black men in terms of pursuing their dreams.

The strong work ethic is hard to find because it is rarely cultivated in Black youth by the adults around them. This is obvious when you look at academic achievement vs. sports. Many of our inner-city youth are bright, intelligent, gifted, and talented; but most of them lack the will, support, and resources necessary to cultivate and hone those gifts for long-term success. Kids who exhibit a talent for sports are encouraged from a young age to work hard, persevere, and think of future goals, but Black youth who are interested in other pursuits such as academics, science, and the arts, not so much. I rarely see kids in urban neighborhoods encouraged to cultivate a strong work ethic in other areas besides sports. I do not see parents making sure Jawan has an opportunity to play the piano, violin, or oboe. I do not see community members showing up in force to encourage Jawan in the school play. I don't see college recruiters showing up at the science fair hoping to spy the next great talent. The resources to experience such things as choir, band or orchestra, or even STEM opportunities are scarce in urban public school districts. Society does not envision youth achieving in these urban areas. Children, youth, and families strive for that brass ring of making it big in sports; dreaming of playing professionally, even though the chances are infinitesimal. They don't realize an equally lucrative career may be achieved in medicine, science, the arts, business, and other fields. Achievement in any of these areas requires a strong work ethic, a desire to work hard, to do what it takes to improve one's self, but it also necessitates opportunity.

RANDALL

Randall was a tremendous athlete in a family of athletes. His brothers all played sports and excelled, one gaining a college scholarship. Randall mainly played sports to hang out with his friends. Sports kept him off of the streets. He had lost a brother to street violence, and he did not want to become another statistic. But this is not what excited him and drove him to excellence. He seemed like a typical sports jock, was a good student, but he was a closet artist. Most people didn't know that about him. It took me a year to realize it. While he participated in his high school's drama program, he craved the opportunity to play significant roles that were never envisioned for guys like Randall. Randall had the desire, the abilities, and the work ethic, but he lacked the opportunity.

Finally, in his senior year, Randall got his chance with the annual spring show. The lead actor fell ill and Randall was asked to fill in for him as well as play his original minor role. For three nights, he played both parts without missing a line. He literally carried the show. My wife and I were there for opening night. The small crowd in attendance loved him. After he graduated, Randall made his own opportunities, participating in local acting programs and workshops. He even produced his own show on the internet. He developed quite a following. He was chosen to act in an internet drama series.

Today, Randall is working a job and preparing for that one big opportunity that will allow him to work as an actor. He continues to participate in drama projects and pursue his other interests in the arts. Despite a lack of encouragement or mentorship as a teenager, Randall cultivated his interest in his craft. Despite attending a school with very limited resources, he had a vision for what he wanted to do and the desire to work hard to accomplish it. I have no doubt that his dream will come to fruition one day.

Delayed self-gratification is the ability to forgo or deny to one's self an immediate benefit or reward for the sake of greater benefit or reward in the future. Practicing delayed self-gratification in the arenas of education, career, and family is the path for gaining the position one wants in life: to cultivate marketable skills, financial options, and economic power. Staying in school, attending classes daily, and working hard for grades in the present will yield rewards later in life for career and educational options, as opposed to dropping out of school to make money selling drugs. When young men practice delayed self-gratification in order to achieve the goals they have in life and pursue their dreams, they can have good outcomes despite their environment.

TONY

I met Tony when he was in fourth grade. His older brother (seventh grade at that time) was on my basketball team and had told me I just had to meet his brother. "My brother is so great at basketball! He's like Kobe Bryant! Nobody can hold him! He can play circles around all the boys on our team." So, I went to the park to see him and his brother was right. He was exceptionally good. The following year, he played on my fifth-grade team, probably the most talented person I ever had play for me. At this point, my teams were playing at the park and recreation level, and he really stood out. Later, he was recruited by and played on AAU teams and was a standout. While many of his peers were running the streets and engaging in self-destructive behavior, Tony surrounded himself with friends who had similar interests and goals. Tony had a goal for his life, to use his skills to make it and get paid so he could help take care of his family.

Tony grew up the fifth of ten children in a family run by a single mom who did a remarkable job of holding the family together. She worked multiple jobs yet gave good attention to her children. My involvement was greatly appreciated by her, since no fathers were around. I had close relationships with all of the boys, engaging them through basketball, mentoring, camps, and such. She would often call Tony or one of his brothers just as we were beginning an activity. She had discovered that they had forgotten to do their chores or failed to do their homework. So, I had to take them back home. Because she would sometimes chew them out in front of their friends for some neglected responsibility, Tony and his brothers were often the butt of jokes and teasing in the group. The other boys thought that she was too strict and overly concerned. I told the group that Tony and his brothers were fortunate to have a mother like that. In actuality, many of the group had parents who were too distracted by their own personal issues to pay attention to what their kids were doing. The greatest tribute to Tony's mom is that out of her ten kids whom she raised, not one of them fell victim to the streets through gang violence, drugs, or jail.

Everybody in his family knew that he was going to get paid one day. He was going to make it as an NBA player. Of course, this was Tony's aspiration, and he worked as hard as he could to get there. He played basketball every chance he got: in the gym, at the park, at school, anywhere he could play. He led his high school team to the state championship. And he didn't slack on the academics. He studied and worked hard at school and made it to college. Unfortunately, a college that recruited him with promises of a starting position on the team reneged on their commitment. By the time this occurred, Tony had passed up opportunities to play elsewhere. It was a hard blow. I was worried that he would quit school. But instead he stayed. He had the maturity to realize that a college education, while it would not afford him fame and riches like an NBA career, would give him a foundation to get a good job and set himself up for a lucrative and satisfying lifestyle. In other words, he could still get paid. Today, he has a good job and is a mainstay of support for his mother.

CATCH-22

Many young Black men are validated for the wrong things, for being tough, hard, or intractable. Demetrius was one of the toughest kids around. He did not fight often, but when he did, few peers could handle him. He gained instant respect wherever he went. Being friends with him was instant credibility. But Demetrius wanted more out of life. He wanted to learn and grow and have a good life. At school all the kids expected him to be rowdy and be their leader in bad behavior but Demetrius didn't want that. He wanted to learn. The "respect" he gained from street kids became a hindrance because it added to teachers' often prejudiced treatment of him. They assumed he was involved in disruptive incidents. They would not challenge him in assignments because they assumed he was not interested in learning.

One day, in his fifth-grade classroom, Demetrius began to weep quietly. His teacher asked what was wrong. He replied that he was frustrated because the behavior of those around him was making it difficult for him to learn in class. It was as if he saw his life flashing before him, going into the dumpster, and he had no control to change it. But he did change it. Demetrius pestered his mom until she transferred him to another school, one in which teachers gave him a chance, did not make negative assumptions about him, and other students were not a distraction. When he was about to go to high school, our program helped him find a private school that would meet his needs and prepare him for college. He applied and was accepted. Today, Demetrius is in college and well on his way to accomplishing his goals of becoming an educated Black man and a positive leader in the community. In order to do this, he had to leave the hood and separate himself from his peers, but often this is what is required of Black boys to break the cycle of poverty and violence in which they are trapped.

Expectations, however, are critical. Black boys receive vindication from their peers for being leaders in negative behavior. They rarely see Black men receiving great adulation from society, except for being athletes and entertainers. There are too few role models of Black men as educators, skilled laborers, businessmen, and so on. It is a catch-22. Whether deserved or not, a Black male may inspire fear in others and resenting it, respond in ways that fulfill the negative expectations, gaining a cheap, quick, false sense of validation, or even acceptance. Many people in the educational system do not expect much from Black children. Low expectations create resentment, distrust, and a devaluation of the educational process, leading to poor academic performance—a fulfillment of those same low expectations. Whether the young people are up to something or not, police are expecting bad behavior, merchants are distrustful, expecting Black people to steal, again causing anger and behavior that invites accusations. A young person will snap (go off, explode); the authorities are called, often leading to negative and violent experiences with the criminal justice system. The Black child has fulfilled all of the expectations of people who find him untrustworthy in the first place. This is the catch-22 of the Black male's existence. Frustration at people's expectations compels action that fulfills them. But like Demetrius, Black boys are often forced to separate themselves from negative influences in order to give themselves a chance at the life they want.

MY OWN CATCH-22

I had taken a small group of Young Lions to a famous restaurant chain for breakfast. We were discussing personal hygiene, proper diet, and health as it relates to African Americans. After we ordered, the manager (a White woman) approached us and asked me if one of the kids had taken a two-dollar tip that she said had been lying on the table. I told her they had not; I was the first person in our group to reach the table and there had been no money lying there. Twice she came back with the same accusation, saying there were witnesses. I asked her to produce the witnesses. She said they had already left the restaurant. Then a busboy (also White) singled out one of our group, who promptly turned his pockets, inside-out. No money! At this point, I asked the manager for an apology, since she didn't have any real reason to suspect anyone in our group. She refused and told me that I needed to teach "these boys" how to behave in a restaurant.

This is when I found myself in a catch-22! I was ready to do the expected— get loud and make a scene! Instead, we rose from our chairs to leave the restaurant. As the boys went out ahead of me, I told the manager that I was angry. Not only were we paying customers, we didn't deserve to be treated in this manner. It didn't make sense to insult customers who were about to spend fifty dollars over a two-dollar tip. She then informed me that she would call the police if I didn't leave. I calmly but firmly told her I wouldn't leave until we had talked this through, so she called the police. The police came, and after they had heard both of our stories, I left, joining the group in the van.

As soon as I got home, I called the regional manager of the restaurant chain; I then drafted a letter. I was so offended I wanted to go back with the boys and as many people as I could get and stage a protest. However, our associate director (my wife) and one of our board members suggested I wait to see how and if the company would respond. The next working day, the regional manager called and expressed regret at how our group was treated at the restaurant. After we haggled with the restaurant for two weeks over a suitable response, our group was invited to the restaurant for a complimentary meal. We also received a personal and public apology from both the manager who committed the offense and the regional manager.

In the *Young Lions* program, our goal is to teach boys what it means to be African American men spiritually, culturally, and physically. Instilling an accurate, strong, and positive self-image by helping boys realize who they are in Christ is the absolute core of this ministry. I repeatedly told the group that I was pursuing this situation because first, they do not have to allow themselves to be mistreated by anyone, and second, they can be angry and use that anger in constructive, nonviolent ways to accomplish their goals, and people will respect that. Although this incident was stressful, time-consuming, and annoying, I was glad that it happened. It became a teaching moment. Through constructive anger, reason, and patience our entire group was accorded the respect we deserved and vindicated for our actions.

CONCLUSION

Getting paid is essentially about the self-worth of the Black male. One way to measure one's worth is to judge how valuable one is to society. In a recent election in Minneapolis, one of the candidates commented that one's monetary value was a good indicator of one's worth to society. Appalling but true! Paychecks, clothes, cars, and even toys have become indicators of one's worth in society's view. This is why clothes, shoes, and other attire are so important to youth—these things are a superficial measure of self-worth. If my possessions are as good as or better than those of my peers, I have a validation of my own self-worth. This is an attitude modeled in every stratum of American society, from the poor to the rarefied atmosphere of superstars and corporate executives. The image one portrays to others through external factors helps assuage self-doubt and low esteem.

Getting paid is a superficial affirmation of one's existence and value. How can I demonstrate my self-worth? How do I prove that I am valuable? How do I justify my existence? In seeking the answers to these questions, young people

97

> ## If the internal measures of self-value do not have meaning, no amount of external acquisitions will result in an abiding sense of self-worth.

need to seek affirmation from someplace besides their external circumstances of where they live, what clothes they wear, how much money they have in their pocket, and so on. If the internal measures of self-value do not have meaning, no amount of external acquisitions will result in an abiding sense of self-worth. Black male youth must learn that they have value because they belong to God and because they are children of God. There is nothing in the world more precious to God. As Paul says in his letter to the Corinthians, "Everything belongs to you . . . but you belong to Christ, and Christ belongs to God" (1 Corinthians 3:21-23).

God sacrificed the life of his only Son to be reunited with Black youth in fellowship. "God so loved the world that he gave his only Son" (John 3:16). If that doesn't make a person feel valuable, I don't know what would! But a lot of young Black men have been sent messages over and over and over again that they do not have value, that they are unworthy, and that they just don't matter: messages from the home, family, peers, society as a whole! Sometimes, they just cannot seem to grasp the fact that God loves them and thinks they are important.

This is where we have to depend on a change of the heart worked by the activity of the Holy Spirit. Sometimes a person has had so much bad stuff dumped on him or her in life that there just is not enough good stuff in the world to pour in to erase it. So we go to a source, which is out of this world, the source of God's love. To internalize the fact that God loves you, that God sacrificed his only son Jesus for you, personally—you can't go any higher than that for vindication, validation, or self-affirmation. There is no higher authority, no higher court, no deeper act of love. There is nothing else anyone can do more than what Christ has already done. All that is left is to believe it—and receive it.

CHAPTER SEVEN
FITTING IN

ANTWAN

Antwan was a lovable and gregarious boy. I watched him grow from a child to adulthood in our ministry. He was a regular in our after-school Bible club and loved going to camp in the summer. He gave his life to Christ and attended church at our house with his family. I have known his family for many years, and have walked beside and prayed with his mother through various crises. While the pressures of the streets and the difficulties of dysfunctional home life turn many children hard and sober, Antwan always seemed in good spirits. His hardships did not seem to get him down. Antwan was so playful and generous in spirit that he lightened the hearts of those in his presence.

His cheerful demeanor belied the stress of the constant struggle his family experienced to meet basic needs for housing, food, and safety. Antwan's family would have to move about once a year due to evictions or substandard living conditions, from one inadequate apartment to another. He lived with his mother, who struggled with mental illness. I think this was the hardest thing Antwan had to deal with because his mother was incapable of giving him the structure and care that he craved. Her attention was erratic and inconsistent. I guess, like for so many other youth, it was this need for attention that led to his getting into trouble so often. Antwan was a follower, so he would do just about whatever the people he was with would tell him to do.

Starting at age eleven, the police began bringing him home from misadventures, such as breaking into someone's house or shoplifting. Invariably, he was the only one picked up, and his story always went like this: he was with a group of his friends and someone suggested he take this shirt from the store, or go in the window of this house, or throw this rock. When accosted, everyone would run and he would get caught. Antwan did not have a malicious bone in his body, but he was always getting into trouble because he would go with whatever crowd he happened to be in—good or bad. Antwan would also fabricate tremendous stories in order to ingratiate himself with others. I would ask, "Antwan, why do you tell those big stories? People already like you, you don't have to tell big lies like that." But Antwan seemed to feel he needed to do that to gain acceptance. He would engage in behavior that he knew was wrong or questionable in order to fit in with his peers. I knew I could keep Antwan on the straight path as long as I could keep him with positive people. Antwan was a *tabula rasa*, a blank slate waiting for whatever influence got to him first. He was a puzzle piece looking for the place where he fit.

HIERARCHY OF NEEDS

Noted psychologist Abraham Maslow theorized a hierarchy of needs (physiological, safety, love/belonging, esteem, and self-actualization) all human beings share. This hierarchy, illustrated by a pyramid with basic needs at the base and culminating with self-actualization at the tip, indicates that every person must have each level of needs met before proceeding to the next level. Basic needs for food, air, and water are an individual's first concern, and then safety, then belonging, then esteem, before a person can achieve fulfillment as an individual. All of these needs are critical for each of us to reach self-actualization, to see ourselves "fitting in" with the grand scheme of things.

People have a fundamental need to be connected to others through relationship. When the young people with whom I work are tempted to gangbang, hang out with a bad crowd, or persist in self-destructive behavior, they are asking, "How do I fit in?" They are expressing this need. At-risk youth experience disconnection in several ways:

- political and economical disenfranchisement due to the socioeconomic boundaries of their neighborhood;
- cultural and racial separation from mainstream society;
- emotional and mental challenges due to fragmented relationships and dysfunction in the home.

If a person learns at a young age that he or she cannot depend on anyone, distrust of others is a given; and as the person matures, relationships are warped as a result. In an ideal world, the family is the place a person finds acceptance and experiences genuine community. However, as we have already seen, the family unit is not always a place of acceptance for many youth. If that basic need is frustrated at a young age, a child could spend a lifetime trying to have that unfulfilled need met, often in negative ways. It is in the context of the community of family that a young person's self-image first forms, for good or bad. If a person is nurtured within the family unit, that person emerges into the broader society confident and secure, contributing to the greater community of humanity. However, if the family unit, through dysfunction, economic stress, and emotional misery becomes a dysfunctional crèche birthing emotionally flawed and suffering individuals, those individuals end up preying on society and being full of resentment because they do not easily find a place to belong or fit in. How do Black males in challenging communities fulfill this basic human need for belonging and finding place?

FITTING IN

Where do male youth in urban neighborhoods find belonging? Many meet this need for belonging and community through negative venues such as gangs. In the gang, estranged youth find acceptance, fulfillment, support, even a form of structure, which may be entirely lacking in their homes. Gang involvement fills a real need that some kids feel, a vacuum of belonging and connection. Often after an occurrence of gang violence, people look at who was involved and comment, "He was such a nice boy. How did he get involved in gangs?" When there is violence involving youth in my community, the catch phrase "gang involvement" or "gang-related" is immediately thrown out by the media or police. When we see otherwise promising youth throwing their lives away by engaging in violent gang activity, we want it to make sense. It's easier to think: "Oh, he was a bad kid." "No wonder he ended up like this. Look at his family." The reality is that a lot of kids who end up involved in gangs are not what you would think of as problem youth. They are just looking for a place to belong.

Taye and his family were some of my earliest friends in the community. As a young boy Taye would do whatever I offered: sports, Bible club, church, after-school activities, anything. He was thirsty for positive attention. His home life was difficult, but he was secure with his brothers and parents. But one day his dad died and Taye changed. He would still do stuff with me, but I had to compete for his attention with a rowdy group of boys. He changed from being a hardworking student to a slacker at school. He dropped out of school before high school and ran the streets with the local gang. Nothing I could do could pull him out of that lifestyle. The gang was his life, his family. One day he was sitting on the steps in front of his friend's house and some rival gang members drove by shooting. It was a hit on Taye and it was successful. He was shot multiple times in his abdomen and chest. By some miracle he survived. When I went to see him he had just come out of surgery. He was surrounded by his fellow gang members, all vowing to retaliate for what had been done to Taye. When he saw me he began crying. He pulled up his shirt and showed me the cross jumble of stitches and cried out, "Look what they did to me, Chris!" And then he grabbed me around the waist and began sobbing. After everyone left, we talked and prayed and he decided that day he was done with the gang life. It was difficult, and sometimes dangerous, but he extricated himself from the gang. He got in a committed relationship and eventually started a family. He now has three sons and is a stalwart of the community.

One family in my neighborhood is notorious for their gang ties and involvement. This connection is their rep in the neighborhood and among the police. It doesn't matter if it's actually true because the police and the media repeatedly report this as fact. Some of their family have died through shootings and suspicious activity, and many of them have been involved in a gang at one

> # Young people try to fit in and gain acceptance among their peers by saying, doing, and being the right and acceptable thing, whether it is moral or not.

time or another. Theirs is a huge extended family network in my community. Five generations of adults and children. They are very close, extremely loyal to one another. If one of them is in trouble, the others rally around that person. The truth is, it would be hard to tell where the family ends and the gang begins. Those who are struggling or walking the wrong side of the law are just as much a core part of the family as those who are "decent" and law-abiding. Family is family and always comes first. Their loyalty and clannishness and refusal to disavow or disown criminal relatives have led them to a lot of grief and soiled reputations. But I tell you what! If you are in this family network, you know you belong. And everyone in the neighborhood knows where you fit in. This belonging—being known, part of something—is what people crave. If you are among the urban poor and are Black, you experience disenfranchisement on many different levels. Belonging and community, needs for all human beings, are valued too highly to jeopardize for mainstream cultural values in which you do not have a place.

Young people try to fit in and gain acceptance among their peers by saying, doing, and being the right and acceptable thing, whether it is moral or not. The clothes a person wears, the people they hang out with, the activities a person engages in are all factors that may gain a young person a form of acceptance among peers. The problem is, they are superficial factors that do not necessarily reflect the real person within, and thus the real need for acceptance for who one is goes unmet. A dynamic of negativity often accompanies the pseudo acceptance found along this path of following the crowd to find acceptance. One example of this is when a group of youth find a point of connection with each other through abusing or mistreating someone else. The following is a scenario common among youth in my urban community.

A small boy was picked on and harassed at school repeatedly. It all came to a head one day at recess when the boy was among a group pushing to get into the building when the bell rang. The boy stumbled and somehow, inexplicably, the crowd of boys turned on him. They began kicking and pushing and stomping him. A mob mentality took over and no one heeded this boy's cries for help. Finally, a boy there saw what was happening and pushed into the crowd and picked the small boy up. After parents and school officials got involved there were immediate consequences. One of the boys singled out for disciplinary action was a boy I worked with. He was active in our after-school ministry and was the last person I would suspect of doing something like this. I asked him how in the world he could ever find himself in a crowd like that, and taking part in that behavior. He replied, "I don't know. I was there and he fell down and someone started kicking him and I just joined in." I wanted to understand how this decent boy could fall into such destructive behavior, but there was no easy, simple, understandable answer for me. The most I could glean is that everyone was doing it so he joined right in.

Youth in urban communities need ways to positively connect with peers. Helping them build positive peer groups with one another is essential for their survival and success. This could be a sports team, a church youth group, a classroom, or any group of young people who share the desire to be positive and affirming. Choosing the right friends is a critical skill for young people. They must find connection with people (youth or adult) who will build them up as maturing adults, rather than spend time with people who want to bring others down to share their brand of misery.

MASS INCARCERATION

American society's message to poor, Black males can be interpreted as: "You don't belong here. You don't belong in this neighborhood, this community . . . you don't belong in our society." So they are relegated to the criminal justice system, and regularly incarcerated in one of America's numerous prisons. Beginning with the so-called war on drugs in the 1970s and '80s, the number of people imprisoned in the United States jumped from three hundred thousand to two million, with Black people having the highest rate of increase. The United States has the highest incarceration rate of any country in the world, imprisoning the largest percentage of its citizens of color. And this, in spite of the fact that it is proven that prison is no deterrent to crime. Black men are sent to prison at a rate some six times greater than that of their White counterparts.[1] The policies adopted to enable America's war on drugs sent many young Black men to prison for minor and nonviolent offenses to serve significant prison terms. The criminal justice system's penalties for the possession or use of crack cocaine, favored by urban Black men, were incredibly more severe than the possession and use of the exact same drug in different form, powder cocaine, favored by White men. One in three Black men in the United States has spent some time in prison. Mass incarceration has become a system of segregation, removing an entire population of people from the sight and mind of American society, and even when released from prison they continue to lead an existence beneath the notice of American society because they are denied basic civil rights for voting and suffer from housing and employment discrimination. Coined by Michelle Alexander as the "New Jim Crow," America's system of mass incarceration effectively separates young Black men from society and denies them basic civil rights.[2] America has essentially found a new way to segregate its Black population from mainstream society through its prison policies.

ZEKE

Like many boys in my neighborhood, Zeke grew up without a father. Also like many of them his father was in prison. The oldest of four children in his mother's household, Zeke never felt like he belonged. Zeke was really short for his age as a preteen, and as he grew older, his peers increased in stature but he remained significantly shorter. He clearly had a chip on his shoulder because of this. His best friend, who was also really short as a preteen but grew to be among the tallest of his peers, confided in me. "I'm worried about Zeke. He feels really bad that he is shorter than everybody else. He's started hanging out with a bad group. He thinks he can get respect by proving he can be as tough as anyone else." At this point, Zeke had been playing on our basketball team for a few years. He had been working on his three-point shot and had just earned the starting shooting guard position on our team. He had prayed to receive Christ during summer camp. But all of a sudden, we didn't see him anymore. He didn't come to practice, games, or any of our activities.

When I talked to his mom, she told me that Zeke had changed; he was out in the street with his new friends all the time. I searched for him and found him. Sure enough, he was with a group hanging out on the corner. I pulled him aside for a visit. He seemed happy, albeit surprised, to see me and promised me he would be back at practice. But he never came back. The next I heard of Zeke he had been imprisoned for breaking and entering with his group of new friends. He followed the pattern of the father who was never in his life. Zeke is a good person at heart, all he wanted was to fit in.

The overwhelming numbers of Black men in prison have an obvious impact on their ability to be at home to contribute financially or emotionally. The shortage of fathers at home due to incarceration has a direct correlation to a host of social issues facing children including school performance and social behavior.

Where do the poor fit in American society? It seems as if being poor is a crime in America. Laws here are not passed to protect or benefit the poor, but the rich. The prison system—our jails, and particularly death row—is not crowded with rich persons but poor. Poor offenders are prosecuted to the fullest extent of the law for engaging in the same illicit behavior that is respected and pardoned in corporate America. Many sources cite that poor people remain in jail because they cannot afford to pay bail. Our "pull yourself up by your bootstraps" society doesn't like to be reminded that many of our citizens do not have boots, much less the figurative "bootstraps," or resources by which one may elevate one's economic condition, or that we have an obligation to those who are economically less fortunate. The poor are ignored and sequestered into "ghettos" where they can be overlooked. That is, until the inevitable overflow of violence and disruption spills into mainstream communities. It is true today more than ever that the rich get richer and the poor just keep getting poorer.

SOCIAL STEREOTYPES

Urban youth struggle to find a place to fit in. Black youth learn from an early age that they do not belong in idealized American society through television shows, ads, movies, and celebrities. Negative stereotypes are propagated in the mainstream media from the evening news to the most popular TV shows. Suspected criminals or otherwise unsavory characters are regular representations of Black manhood in the media, the regular exceptions being the professional athlete or the popular entertainer. Negative stereotypes abound. The idea that the only way a Black person can achieve mainstream acceptance is through sports or entertainment is a negative and demeaning stereotype. We rarely see images of Black men in the media who have gained recognition because of years of hard work or success in business, technology, or other non-entertainment fields. Black men who live decent, productive lives but are not rich or famous are subject to the ravages of institutional racism, an unjust judicial system, abuse by the police, and street violence. The representation of positive Black manhood, realistic to everyday life, on television, the media, or even movies, is relatively scarce.

The images that are spotlighted are not often those that are suitable by Christian standards for young viewers to emulate. Many rap and hip hop artists and professional athletes lead lifestyles that are self-serving and often self-destructive, but apparently it's acceptable because they are rich and famous. These negative role models do more harm than if there were no models at all in the media for Black manhood. Black youth glorify the lifestyles of these pretenders, who pretend like they have a fulfilling life. Black boys see them and they want to be just like them. They want to be rich, they want to have lots of girls hanging all over them, they want to live lifestyles of material gluttony with gold chains hanging off their necks; fat, bejeweled rings encumbering their fingers; and a fleet of fancy cars at their disposal. The urban version of the American dream. They think that's cool. But most of these pretenders are just flashes in the pan, often ending up poor, dead, or in jail, succumbing to the same socio-economic pressures surrounding the poor children who want to emulate them.

At the same time we regularly read in the news about superstar athletes who got paid, making millions of dollars a year, yet ending up in bankruptcy court or being sued for child support or going to jail for committing crimes of assault or abuse, or even murder. They never grew up, you see. They are still trying to figure out how they can fit in. The acquisition of wealth and material possessions is a primary way youth try to fill the need for belonging. The drive to acquire money and possessions is simply a means to fit in, or validate one's existence. Young people in the city are constantly barraged with messages about the haves and have-nots in America. People with money and possessions are people of worth, while people who are poor are beneath the notice of society. Advertisements and media messages drive this message home continuously. Immediate self-gratification fuels the drive for material acquisitions. The acquisition of material possessions produces immediate gratification although it is tenuous, slight, and temporary, until the next popular trend comes along. But it makes people feel good, like they belong, like they are somebody.

Immediate self-gratification shortchanges a person of the patience, wisdom, and lasting satisfaction that comes from working toward and achieving a goal. As Black youth learn who they are in Christ, their attitudes about material possessions will change. They will no longer feel validated by what they wear or own. Their validation will come from a sense of who they are on the inside, as children of God, not from how successfully they conform to the world's standards. They will learn they don't have to engage in self-destructive behavior, such as committing crimes, engaging in violence, or doing drugs, to fit in. As they reorient their behavior to match their values as children of God, they will find life-affirming ways to belong and gravitate to others like themselves. Their sense of belonging will be connected to their sense of who they are on the inside. Seeing themselves differently as children of God provides a needed boost to self-esteem and will help them craft an accurate, positive self-image, which will prevent them from falling prey to negativity and despair.

The ideal American profile is to be affluent and materialistic, from which it then follows that you are White. If you are Black and poor, you suffer from the double whammy of racism and classism, leading to a poor and distorted self-image. Self-image drives all other motivations in life. When self-image is distorted or negative, then so is a person's outlook on life. Due to social and familial dysfunction and pressures, many disadvantaged people struggle with a negative self-image. This is manifested most often by young Black males in their treatment of others. Low self-esteem leads to self-hatred. Self-hatred results in a myriad of negative behaviors among Black youth including poor attitudes toward school and education, lack of self-control, unfettered anger, a lack of respect for others and their possessions, and self-destructive and violent tendencies. Self-hatred manifests itself in chemical abuse, violence, and other forms of self-abuse and leads to the abusive treatment of others. This abuse may take the form of physical violence or verbal abuse, but it reflects a deep hatred of self transferred to another. Taking advantage of someone who is weaker is a cheap way to feel strong.

Discipleship of Black male youth must include teaching them that they are valuable because they are God's creation. They need to trust that they have value and importance to the eternal God, and thus they mean something and life itself has meaning. With that grounding, they may develop an accurate and positive self-image as they see themselves as children of God. Learning who one is in Christ will produce self-esteem and respect and enable one to view others with consideration and respect.

CONCLUSION

To the young man who suffers from fragmented relationships, isolation, and distrust, Christ imparts healing and a sense of community. The primary relationship of each individual must be with God through Christ. Through this relationship with God all other relationships may be redeemed and yield true fulfillment. When youth learn who they are in Christ, they experience belonging, they know where and how they fit in. The blood of Jesus has healed the rift between God and people caused by sin. As community has been restored with God through the work of Christ, interpersonal relationships may be healed so that we may experience connection with one another through Christ. Interpersonal relationships and human community become sacred places in which Christ may dwell. Others are seen in a different light, and relationships take on a holy aspect as an extended means of relating to God. Young people can break from the cycles of intergenerational poverty to relate to themselves, others, and society in a new, redeeming way. But it starts with the individual. This is a complete paradigm shift in how relationships are viewed in all of human society, not just in the inner city. Relationships with self and others change in light of the implications of the individual's relationship with God.

Youth need to know that they belong. In their families, among their peers, in society . . . they belong. They do not have to wander in this world looking for a place to fit in, they belong to God. This is the first and foremost truth of their lives as children of God. Although they may be estranged in mainstream society, they are not aliens and strangers in God's kingdom but citizens. They are not out of place in this world if they are connected to God; rather, it is this world that is out of place with God. It is those who are separated from God who are lacking genuine community. As children of God, young people have a place to go in Christ, they have a place to fit in in Christ, they have a community to which they belong in Christ. The Church must step up and offer avenues of community and spiritual growth and identity for our youth. This sense of community, connection, and belonging begins with the knowledge of who they are in Christ. It begins with a deep, abiding assurance that they are not alone, but God and Christ are always with them. They will appreciate positive opportunities to grow and experience community through friends, church, and family. They can resist the temptation to behave in immoral and self-destructive ways in order to curry favor with their peers. They do not have to struggle to fit in anymore, because they know who they are in Christ.

From this point of self-knowledge they may proceed to accomplish any task in life that is before them. The sense of belonging they gain through Christ and the Church will enable them to overcome obstacles to proceed toward self-actualization and fulfillment. Antwan, as desperate as he is, can thumb his nose at the world that shuns him, because he belongs to Christ. Jesus said, "In the world you have distress. But be encouraged! I have conquered the world" (John 16:33). In this world the urban Black male may have nothing: no status, no wealth, no real connection with anyone; but in Christ he has everything. The self-affirmation that comes from identifying with Christ can be parlayed into the will and discipline to put his life together, one piece at a time. Jesus told Peter and the disciples, "I assure you that anyone who has left house, brothers, sisters, mother, father, children, or farms because of me and because of the good news will receive one hundred times as much now in this life—houses, brothers, sisters, mothers, children, and farms (with harassment)—and in the coming age, eternal life" (Mark 10:29-30). If Antwan, or any young, estranged Black male, would submit his life to Christ, he would begin to experience victory over the trials that besiege his self-esteem. Instead of living to survive each day and trying to get by working whatever angles or shortcuts he can figure out, he can take charge of his life, and God will make it better than he could imagine! The problems that grow over a lifetime of abuse and suffering will not disappear overnight, but God proclaims, "I am making everything new!" (Revelation 21:5 NIV).

CHAPTER EIGHT
Being Black

"THIS LOOKS LIKE A WHITE PERSON'S HOUSE"

One day our doorbell rang and I opened my door to an eleven-year-old boy named Ray Ray. Youth in the neighborhood were always dropping in on me and my family for a random visit (to talk, play some games, get something to eat). He came in and looked around and said, "This looks like a White person's house." I laughed and asked him why he thought that. He said it was because it was clean and neat. I said, "So you're saying that Black people's houses can't be clean?" And he said, "Yeah," and looked at me like I didn't have any sense. I wondered about this simple exchange for days.

It's been years since it happened and the memory of it influences me daily in my work with youth. Why would Ray Ray think that Black people live in dirty houses, while White people live in clean ones, much less the negative extensions: Black people don't clean their houses? Black people don't take care of things? Black people don't have anything nice? The comment didn't cause Ray Ray any sense of shame. It was, to him, a statement of fact. This was how he saw the world, his reality, all he knew, his home and the homes of his friends and associates, living in the neighborhood. When I visited in Ray Ray's home, I began to understand his worldview. In Ray Ray's house, chemical abuse was present and basic needs were going unmet. When you opened the door to his apartment building, you were struck with the smell of urine. The apartment itself had been dirty and unkempt with the pervading smell of funky clothes piled up in corners (dirty mixed with clean), dirty dishes stacked up, children sleeping on couches, floors, and dirty mattresses, the litter of empty beer and liquor containers, and garbage overflowing trash containers. This was normal to Ray Ray—all of his friends lived in similar circumstances.

My house was an alien environment to him. The state of his house was not a reflection of skin color, nor of poverty. I'd been in many homes in my neighborhood that were well-kept and clean, in spite of their poverty. A home in which the adult is working multiple jobs to make ends meet is not likely to allow that home to descend into squalor. A parent who is going to such extremes to care for her or his family is going to enlist the aid of their children to share in the upkeep of the house and show responsibility. Many families have no choice but to live in substandard conditions dictated by slum landlords and devastating economic conditions. It can be difficult for some families to maintain cleanliness in heart and life in the face of a poverty that permeates a person's world until it debases a person in spirit as well as social status. The spiritual malaise accompanying debilitating poverty influences every part of a person's life and psyche, fundamentally affecting people's perception of themselves and the world around them.

I have been in homes of White families who were equally debased, but they did not equate the state of their poverty with the color of their skin. Yet being poor and the presence of self-abuse in the family influenced this boy's concept of what it means to be Black. As a society, in many ways, in our institutions and social contacts, we perpetuate the inferiority complex of Black children instilled through generations of slavery and inhumane treatment. Every discriminatory practice our children and youth experience in school, with police, in social settings reinforces this false and debilitating message. The self-abasement and fundamental retardation of self-concept, which comes with living in poverty, is stark. By contrast, I also spent my early, formative years in a segregated, low-income community, yet I did not suffer the spiritual malaise that I find in my neighborhood now. My concept of being Black derived from family members whose values of discipline, hard work, and respect for self were passed on to me. These values, particularly when I encountered racism or prejudice, enabled me to overcome significant barriers in my life to education, career, and self-fulfillment. These are values that many of our Black youth growing up in urban areas today lack.

"IS THIS YOUR GIRLFRIEND?"

The same issue crops up when kids first meet my wife and children. "Is this your girlfriend?" The worldview of young Black men in the hood in regard to family is also impacted by decades of poverty and by a welfare system that has long encouraged Black men to stay away from their families to allow the mother and children's eligibility to receive financial assistance from the government. In their world, men do not marry the women with whom they have babies. In fact, in my neighborhood most young Black fathers do not have wives; they have baby mamas. Consequently, the assumption is that I am not married to the woman who is the mother of my child. The comment was not made from any malicious or accusatory motive, but from friendly, childish curiosity. Yet, this is another sentiment that causes me to wonder. For them—what is the norm in regards to family formation? The phrase "daddy, mommy, and baby make three" does not seem to apply. Many times, young people will come into my house and not even speak to my wife. I teach the boys to address the woman of the household when they enter out of respect, and I take pains to introduce my wife as my wife, if they do not already know her. Upon introduction, their eyes will widen in surprise as if to say, "You're married?"

To them, I'm a novelty. I'm out of place in their worldview. They don't mean any disrespect, they just haven't been shown any other way. Another disturbing revelation came when some told me one day that I need to keep my wife in check by hitting her now and then. They had decided that something wasn't right in my relationship with my wife because when I was out with them, I would check in with her to let her know where I was. They thought I needed to remind her who was in charge by slapping her around. What they perceived as a controlling wife was unheard of in their houses. The men in their lives certainly wouldn't allow their girlfriends or baby mamas to put such restraint on them. They were full of all kinds of helpful advice for me. I shouldn't have to check in with my wife or let her know where I'm going when I leave the house. Checking in with one's spouse before making plans was not a sign of mutual respect, but of weakness and insubordination. They would never allow their girlfriends or anyone to disrespect them in any way or else they'd "go off" (act violently). I realized that for these boys to have positive ideals of Black fatherhood and being a Black husband, I had to first deconstruct their pervasive negative images.

Why do so many young Black men in the hood grow up with these assumptions?

- Black people are poor.
- Black people live in dirty houses.
- Black people do not take care of their possessions.
- Black men do not marry the women with whom they have children.
- To take any disrespect from a woman is disgraceful.
- It is acceptable to use violence against a woman.

And how can we deconstruct this pervasive, negative self-image?

I am surprised at the specific behavior that constitutes Blackness among children. The boys I work with often question my Blackness because I don't lie, don't cheat, don't steal, am not promiscuous, and I use proper English (most of the time). What is interesting is that although my Blackness is often challenged on account of these behaviors, which don't conform to their experience, my Blackness is never questioned based on the time I spend in the community and the effort I make to come alongside them in their experiences every day. They rarely see adults who invest time and build relationships with children. There were many instances when I would comfort one of my own crying children or coddle a baby and I would be accused of spoiling that child. In the experience of these boys, Black men are not nurturers.

WHAT DOES IT MEAN TO BE BLACK?

When boys first visit me at my house, it is definitely a cultural shock. I don't do the things they expect a Black man to do. My behavior shakes up their worldview, the way they see themselves and others around them. Like all adolescents, they are asking the eternal question, "Who am I?" Like all adolescents, they formulate answers to this question from their home, family, and social environments. They are seeking answers to this question culturally, physically, and spiritually. Culturally, boys have a need to understand their Blackness. In the context of a society that often fears and distrusts them because of the color of their skin, coming to terms with their own self-identity is critical in the social development of an African American boy. For them, this need is compounded by all the socioeconomic baggage that comes with being Black and poor. They have to contend with the attitudes and suppositions of the broader mainstream society that views the whole population through general, negative stereotypes, which they have often internalized through self-denigrating and self-destructive attitudes and behaviors, turning fear, anger, and angst in upon itself.

I often take groups of boys out on a trip to other cities to broaden their worldview. On one trip, we passed a movie rental store. One of the boys suggested that we go in and rent a movie. I told him it was a bad idea because we were just stopping for lunch, then leaving town; how could we ever return the movie? He looked at me like I was ignorant and said, "Chris, we're Black!" In essence he was saying, "Chris, I have no plan to return it. That's what people expect of us, so that's what we do." I wasted no time in sharing with him my disapproval of that attitude and the shame he was bringing on himself, his family, and Black people in general.

I found a different attitude among the poor when I made a trip to East Africa. I visited homes in the Mathare Valley slums of Nairobi, Kenya. It was an emotionally trying experience in which we were required to have an armed escort. I felt I was participating in one more message of debasement being sent to the poor by mainstream society. My heart and mind ached as I imagined how people felt in this community as they saw us escorted past their homes by armed soldiers. Though I'd read about slums in underdeveloped countries, the Mathare slums were worse than I could imagine; nothing compares to seeing and experiencing them firsthand. My senses reeled from smells and sights that filled me with revulsion; yet, people welcomed us into their homes and treated us like honored guests. People lived in homes built from corrugated tin and

115

cardboard, crammed together with barely room to pass between them. In this place, where sewage ran down the middle of the passageways between homes, and flies buzzed on food, filth, and children's faces alike, I saw God.

As we passed down one passageway, hopping back and forth over the foul water running down the middle, I heard singing and worship and praise to God. I stopped to look in the window of a dwelling and the room was filled with people singing praises to God—it was a church! In the front of the room a man stood preaching and exhorting the roomful of people. I was hushed and awed in my spirit to see God in this place. I met a young boy and his father who lived here. They invited us into their home to visit. There were six people in our group and only three of us could enter because there was not enough room for everyone in their abode. Of the five of us in the house, including the boy and his father, only two of us had places to sit.

As the boy began to share with us through an interpreter, I looked at my surroundings and grew more and more amazed at his story. In spite of his grossly destitute surroundings, this boy attended school every day and made good grades. He was on track to earn a scholarship to college. His father works and saves money in hopes of moving his family to a better place someday. The boy works as well and contributes money toward this goal. They were not angry, bitter, or resentful, but determined to improve their situation in life. They were not cowed by their circumstances, but saw a good future for themselves. This boy had a strong sense of who he is and what he could accomplish if he worked hard in life. Such hope is scarce among the urban poor in American cities where the burden of poverty often drives people to self-destructive and debased behavior.

The stigmatization of poverty is different here in the United States than in other countries. In America, the poor are blamed for their poverty. Individuals and whole ethnicities are accused of being lazy, unambitious, criminal, morally corrupt, and so on. There is seldom consideration given to the thought that people are often subject to circumstances beyond their control, or Lord forbid, that our American way of life necessitates that there exists a lower class. While absolute poverty is clearly more pronounced in developing countries, the effect of relative poverty, compared to our own standard of living, has a more deleterious effect on the individual and communal psyche. In truth, many Americans considered poor here could be considered solidly middle class in other countries. In other countries, people can be poverty-stricken but still consider themselves as part of mainstream society. A person may be homeless, sleeping in alleys each night but wake in the morning and go to work to a respectable job. The attitude of American society toward unemployment itself contributes to the stigma of being poor; if you have no job, you have no social worth. You deal with the double whammy of the stigma of being poor and of systemic racism toward Black people. This inevitably leads to a dearth in self-image and self-esteem and leads to self-destructive behavior and choices.

The question of what it means to be Black is a loaded one for youth. The search for knowledge of self and culture as a Black person is weighted with presumptions and assumptions based on environment. The concept of Blackness may mean and look different to someone who lives in the country in the South, versus someone living in the inner city, versus someone living in the suburbs. For many, the quest for self-identity is limited to the experience of growing up in the hood. Finding ways to expose young people to Black life and culture beyond the ten square blocks of their immediate neighborhood must be an integral part of ministry to them. Their knowledge of what it means to be Black must be informed by both engagement with African Americans with a wide range of experience and socioeconomic status and a more holistic experience of the history and culture of African American people.

BLACK HERITAGE AND SPIRITUALITY

For young Black men growing up in the inner city, the hood is your world. Ray Ray assumed that all Black people were poor; all the ones he knew were poor. This was not only a poverty in goods, but a poverty in spirit. He thought this was all there was for him in life. Sure, there are Black celebrities but they don't count. They are in a different world, which because of their money and fame gives them more commonality and acceptance in the ranks of mainstream American society. The Black middle class has been criticized for abandoning the urban communities from which they sprang, but more and more in American cities, Black middle-class families are returning and making their presence felt in positive ways. At Park Avenue Church in South Minneapolis, where I

> **The values of community, connectedness, and communal spirituality are inherent in Black culture, in contrast to the individualized, fragmented, material possession–based values of mainstream American society.**

first began this ministry many years ago, a significant number of Black families (two-parent households) moved into the neighborhood and bought homes. This had a tremendous impact on the Church's voice and its ministry in the community. I purposed to bring the children from the community in contact with the men from these families so that Black boys could see a different life for themselves. In order for Ray Ray to have a broader idea of self-image, he needs to know his heritage and how the contributions of Black people have played an integral role in making our country great. He needs to see and be exposed to Black families who are not poor and African Americans in various occupations so that he knows that being poor is not part and parcel to being Black. He needs to see people who look like him going to work every day, raising a family, and engaging in positive, uplifting activities. He needs to know that family stability is not just about money and profession. He needs to know that in spite of all the socioeconomic factors we inherit, being Black is a rich fount of heritage, cultural pride, and strength and that Black people possess a deep spirituality inherent through a history of struggle and suffering.

Black African heritage extends centuries before European contact. It is artistically rich with cultural values of respect for life, honor of family, and duty to self at the core of a vibrant lifestyle. The values of community, connectedness, and communal spirituality are inherent in Black culture, in contrast to the individualized, fragmented, material possession–based values of mainstream American society. These values empowered New World Africans to survive through centuries of the horrific existence of slavery. Their spirituality, enlightened by the gospel of Christ, enabled them to rise above the false integrity of the religion of their masters and owners to draw near to the

God of all oppressed people. Nevertheless, the tension between Afrocentric and Eurocentric values contribute to the stress and dysfunction experienced by Black families in America.

The struggle of African Americans for a place of equality and respect in American society was a struggle waged with the strength borne of personal trial, community identity, and support and dependence on God for deliverance from evil. The civil rights struggle was a contest between good and evil, right and wrong. The civil rights movement was based on the spiritual values of nonviolent resistance and civil disobedience, incorporated by Dr. King, James Lawson, and Ella Baker and embraced by the college students who led sit-in demonstrations in North Carolina and Tennessee, the Freedom Riders who risked their lives to desegregate bus stations in the South, and many people of diverse faiths and ethnicities all over the country. The spiritual vigor of Black people tipped the balance of the scales of justice so that the civil rights movement was victorious. The lessons and practices (training, prayer, song, preaching, exhortation) of the civil rights movement are crucial aspects of Black cultural identity. Young Black men must know their heritage, so that they see their connectedness with something greater than themselves and learn to appropriate the spiritual strength that resides within them in times of need.

"WHY DID GOD MAKE ME BLACK?"

The experience of being Black and poor makes youth feel like the pariahs of American society. Due to an impoverished spirit, many are prompted to ask: "Why did God make me Black?" As if being Black was a punishment. Like Ray Ray, many feel that being Black is inferior to being White. Because of institutional racism and systemic injustice, being Black is a substandard caste in American society. Slavery was justified on the basis of dehumanizing Africans. The Constitution refers to them as being three-fifths human. White slaveholders claimed they were saving them by enslaving them. They quoted scripture to demonstrate that Blacks as a people were cursed by God. In the case of Dred Scott, the United States government defined them as being property and not qualifying for citizen rights. Poor Black people are dehumanized today in many subtle ways in our enlightened society through being denied access to housing, employment, education, politics, and other areas essential to American citizenship and livelihood. We live in a time where police, or anyone claiming they feel threatened, can shoot down Black men in the street, with little fear of reprisal or consequence. Many states have instituted Stand Your Ground laws that allow people to shoot someone only on the basis of feeling threatened. This sparked a spate of violence against Black boys and men beginning with Trayvon Martin (2012), and which continues to this day with the brutal killing of Ahmaud Arbery (2020). And somehow this law stands because our society accepts the idea that Blacks as a people are inherently inferior to Whites; a notion that has flourished in mainstream America for centuries and continues to exist.[1] Some Black people have fallen victim to it and, ironically, act in ways that reinforce this false notion.

BEING BLACK IS NOT A CURSE, IT IS A BLESSING

James H. Cone is known as the founder/father of Black Liberation Theology. His views on how an oppressed people see God gives valuable insight on how to help Black youth craft a positive self-image. In *A Black Theology of Liberation*, he addresses the question of the nature of God in the light of the oppression that Blacks have endured in America. He explains: God is Black. His definition of the term *Blackness* is not about the color of a person's skin, but includes any individual or group of people suffering under oppression by social structures. Cone's claim that God is Black is not to engage in an anthropomorphic conception of God, but rather that the quality of Blackness originates with God. All people need to become Black with God. We all need this fundamental quality of liberation, an identification with the suffering in the world.

This view stands in contrast with the perception in mainstream culture that God is White. A "White" God is a God of the privileged. The God of Black Theology is a God on the side of the oppressed. To know God is to be on the side of the oppressed. It is inconceivable that God could condone the behavior of oppressors that leads to the suffering of a people; it is against God's own nature (Luke 4:18; Isaiah 1:17; Psalm 103:6; Proverbs 22:22-23; Zechariah 7:10). This is not to say that suffering gives an individual or people free rein with God, but there is something about suffering and experiencing oppression that allows one to be open and vulnerable to God and his working. Jesus himself, God's own Son, learned obedience through his experience of suffering (Hebrews 5:8).

The miracle of the faith of enslaved people who practiced the religion of Jesus better than the oppressors who taught them is astounding. The Christian gospel tapped into an innate spirituality of the Africans who were stolen from their homeland and enabled them to embrace its truth in spite of the cruelty and hypocrisy of the slaveholders, who used religion to pacify the enslaved. Despite being seen as less than human, Black people had a truer soul that perceived the glories of heaven as they sang their spirituals infused with a hope and joy, which oppression could not destroy. They knew that their masters' practice of religion was hypocritical and proved themselves closer in spirit to God through their suffering.

Black spirituality is a different animal altogether from White spirituality. Black spirituality is a spirituality that overcomes. It has evolved from African spirituality, which embraced and was transformed by the gospel of Christ, to become the life's blood of an oppressed people. It has been honed through generations of suffering and oppression. It is a spirituality that overcomes and does not succumb. It is a spirituality that has as its focus God, who stands on the side of the oppressed and not the oppressors; God who despises oppression in any shape or form. The Black Church as its agency has been a stalwart of strength, patience, and grace in the face of struggle, as well as otherworldly militancy in times of social change. The Black Church has nurtured its people through oppression beyond the capacity of the human spirit to conceive, from the lynching of Emmett Till to the slaughter of Black saints just years ago at the hands of a White supremacist while gathering for Bible study and prayer in the sanctuary of their church. This is the historical spirituality that is the birthright of our young Black men. It must be restored to the poor Black family experience and drawn upon for families and youth in urban areas in order to overcome the trials and issues they face daily in a world that fears and distrusts them. In my experience, young men are hungry for a spirituality that affirms who they are culturally. They must draw upon this innate spirituality in order to overcome the trials and struggles they face daily in the inner city. They must realize that being Black is not a curse, but a blessing.

BLACKNESS IS A GIFT FROM GOD

Those who would disciple Black male youth must be cognizant of these issues and aware of their own misconceptions and attitudes about Black people and Black spirituality. Leaders must have as their goal to help young Black men develop an accurate and positive image. Black male youth growing up in the city must cast off negative paradigms of what it means to be Black, rejecting the oppressive views of mainstream society. Leaders must help youth accept and embrace that Blackness is from God. Blackness is good, because God created everything good. Through the extended African American community, Black youth may learn to appreciate their culture and the great heritage to which they belong, and thus aspire to great things. Because this is how God made them, this is who they are in Christ. Being Black means

- being resilient in the face of suffering and trying times;
- possessing a tremendous reservoir of inner strength;
- overcoming and surviving obstacles;
- thriving in taking on life's challenges;
- possessing a deep spirituality that produces resilience;
- standing on the shoulders of those who have gone before.

There is a richness in being Black, an inheritance of strength and resilience. As these young men seek fulfillment, satisfaction, and self-respect, they must cultivate a true understanding of who they are and respect for their value to God.

IT TAKES GOD TO BE A BLACK MAN

The theme of my ministry among Black boys in North and South Minneapolis is that they belong to God. It is to realize, and help them realize, that their Blackness, their being male, comes from God, and therefore it is good. They do not have to succumb to racist expectations or negative stereotypes, because Blackness is good. God is the author and creator of Blackness, and everything God created is good. So young Black men are inherently good and their culture is good, regardless of what society might say. There is no true Blackness apart

122

from God. Cultural expression, language, dress, behavior, and so on should honor God or it is not truly part of being Black. Blackness is not a construct of society, but derives from God's own self. No matter how popular the latest trend may be, no matter what someone thinks "Black people" do, if God is not in it, it cannot be truly Black. Negative stereotypes do not define Blackness. Bad habits or unhealthy behavior may be present in the life of a Black individual, but none of these aspects, in and of themselves, constitute being Black. To be strong, healthy, positive, and to honor God, this is what it means to be a Black man. To be authentically Black, you have to be connected to the source of Blackness, regardless of social or economic status. It takes God to be a Black man! A strong and spiritual Black man is a unique and special wonder in the world. A Black man of God cannot be subjugated, abused, manipulated, or enslaved. Whatever occurs around him, his spirit is with God. Being a Black man of God is countercultural, both to mainstream society and often to what we call Black culture itself. This is why a Black man needs God; he cannot be authentically Black without God. A Black man depends on God to make it in this world. God is a Black man's strength. The Ray Rays of the world need God in order to be strong Black men.

CHAPTER NINE

IN CHRIST

TYREE

Tyree was involved in our ministry from his childhood and as an adult attended church regularly. Though unmarried, he is a father now, and very attentive to his son and his parental responsibilities. When young, though immersed in the street lifestyle and hampered by the problems facing black young men in urban neighborhoods, he avoided getting into serious trouble. He has been on a path of seeking God since he was young as a result of his involvement with our ministry. He played basketball with us and was particularly attached to his coach, who also mentored him. Though bad choices prevented him from taking advantage of the opportunity to attend college and play football immediately after high school graduation, he dealt with the consequences of those choices and is now about to get his college degree with a teaching accreditation. I have a lot of respect for him for that.

Every Sunday that he is at church, Tyree regales us with stories of his wild days. I marvel as he frankly relates the difficulties he faced growing up in the hood, and how if it wasn't for the people God put in his life, he would not have made it. Tyree is just on the brink of having a good and stable life. He is so close. But Tyree has problems. Between losing his job, being evicted, and learning that he may have another child on the way, he is struggling right now to keep his head above water. But he hasn't given up. I keep expecting to hear at any time that he has quit school, but he hasn't. I expect him to stop coming to church, but he still comes. He just keeps on pushing on. He keeps calling and stopping by. I've known a lot of young men who when things get hard lose their faith in God, but he keeps coming to church and keeps praying. He keeps hoping. He is staying in school and he hasn't forsaken his son. He holds on to his hope that things will get better. He comes to me frequently for aid and advice, but I can't fix things for him. All I can tell him is to work hard, don't give up, and trust in God.

After I had grown to adulthood, I came back to my old neighborhood to visit Mrs. Luke, the woman who led me to Christ. This is what she told me: "Chris, of all the kids in the youth group, you were the one who, once you started following Jesus, you never looked back." Her affirmation summed up my spiritual walk. I was not the leader of our group, nor the smartest or even the most spiritual, but I clung to Christ. Since I invited Christ into my life kneeling at the altar at my church with Mrs. Luke by my side, I have never looked back. I have never considered that God was not real or that Christ did not live inside of me or that I would not have eternal life. I bought into all of it, and it changed my entire life. Through hard times and good times my faith remained constant. Once I discovered who I was in Christ, nobody could tell me anything different.

The legacy I want to leave behind through this ministry is not young Black men with picture-perfect lives, without problems, who are good all the time, but men who hope, who trust in God no matter their current circumstances, who know who they are in Christ, who, when they fall on hard times, pick themselves up and keep moving forward through their faith in God. When young men know who they are in Christ, they can handle any circumstance, no matter the obstacle before them.

For many like Tyree, it is often a relatively insignificant obstacle, for example, a lack of money—too often a relatively small amount—that will keep them from pursuing their goals. For anyone with a middle-class background who is struggling, there is often some family, relative, or friend who can help out with financial assistance or a small loan; but many young Black men who grow up in the city do not know anyone who has money or resources. They do not know people who can lend them money. They are tempted by opportunities of getting money quick through criminal or unethical means. It may be one seemingly insurmountable issue that causes them to give up and quit. They have no support system to back them up when they hit a wall. They do not know people who have been through the same struggle and made it, who can encourage them and give them advice or who may advocate or intercede on their behalf. They feel totally alone in their struggle.

There is no quick and easy road to emotional and financial stability, but if they know who they are in Christ, there is no doubt in their hearts that they will get there. They realize that God is in control and can be trusted with every area of their lives. They are not alone. The faith they need to get through the hard times is not only faith that God will give them eternal life, but faith that God will help them achieve their goals in this life. As Jesus said in John 10:10, "The thief enters only to steal, kill, and destroy. I came so that they could have life—indeed, so that they could live life to the fullest."

IN CHRIST

My vision for men and boys growing up in the hood is grounded in the apostle Paul's exposition in Ephesians. They must be aware, on a fundamental level, that they belong to the Lord, realizing that they are in Christ, and Christ is in them. They are a part of each other in communion—it's a package deal. Indeed, apart from Christ, they cannot attain to the splendor and glory of who they are meant to be as children of God. They need Christ to be authentically Black, authentically male, and to achieve success and satisfaction in life. Knowing who they are in Christ means that young Black men are aware of their spiritual position in the universe by way of their relationship with Christ.

In him we were also chosen, having been predestined
according to the plan of him who works out everything
in conformity with the purpose of his will, in order that
we, who were the first to put our hope in Christ, might be

*for the praise of his glory. And you also were included in
Christ when you heard the message of truth, the gospel
of your salvation. When you believed, you were marked in
him with a seal, the promised Holy Spirit, who is a deposit
guaranteeing our inheritance until the redemption of those
who are God's possession—to the praise of his glory.*

(Ephesians 1:11-14 NIV)

Christ is over everything, and those who believe are in Christ. By faith through grace, not by our own merits or worthiness, believers enjoy a unique and favored position as co-inheritors of the Kingdom because we are *in Christ*. Not because we have earned it, but because we are *in Christ*. It's because of what Jesus did on the cross. For the young Black man in the hood,

- in Christ, he is reconciled to God;
- in Christ, he is forgiven;
- in Christ, he has new life;
- in Christ, all things are under him; nothing can stand up to him.

The young Black male believer in Christ cannot be overcome by the world's circumstances or environment. In Christ, he sees things differently, feels things differently, relates to things differently. He is moving from a position of power and strength, not victimization. In Christ, he is truly a new creation, something the world has not seen, does not know about, and cannot understand. To know who you are in Christ is to be immersed in the personality and power of God by his Holy Spirit. This is a 24/7, 365-day reality. And it influences and impacts every thought, choice, and decision. We are never without him or apart from him. To instill this unique and fundamental sense of identity is necessary in discipling youth. They must realize that their Blackness, their culture, their essential identity come from God, requiring a paradigm shift in how they see themselves.

POTENTIAL OF YOUNG BLACK MEN

As I walk beside the young people in our ministry, I see their potential, despite their environment and behaviors. I know that they are precious to God and worthy of investment. They are God's children; God has not forsaken them, but has great plans for them. Yes, this population is often born into a quagmire of poverty and racism, but God's plan is to extricate them, according to God's will and pleasure. They have only to embrace God's love and plan for them to extricate themselves and step into God's purpose for their lives. God has great love for them and makes them alive in Christ, heirs to the riches in glory that come with being a child of God, this in spite of their obvious shortcomings and in spite of their demeaning environment.

This is the gospel for all humanity, but the God of the oppressed holds out a hand to all Black kids, saying, "Come, follow me. Let me lift you up out of this mess and show you who you really are." By clinging to Christ, they are indeed seated in the heavenly realms with Christ, even as they endure police harassment and shootings, oppression and abuse, racist individuals and institutions, as well as the ravages of poverty. In spite of all these things, they can stand tall, strong, and true in Christ. Knowing who they are in Christ is a gift from God that empowers them to step into their potential, in fulfillment of their creation, not as the dregs of society, but to be its light, and to serve God by doing good works. Although in American society they are often despised and overlooked as being strangers and outcasts, in a deeper and truer sense they belong to God. They belong to God's plan for the universe and that belonging supersedes all temporary and social belonging, because this belonging and inclusion is eternal. God's plan for them is at the center of the salvation of our society, our world, and of all humanity.

LIVING POWERFULLY

Young urban Black men can live powerful lives "worthy of the call you received from God" (Ephesians 4:1). They should live in a manner befitting that of children of God. Out of ignorance concerning the nature of true Blackness, they often interpret the qualities of respect toward others—studiousness, kindness—as trying to act White. They must be dissuaded of this attitude, understanding that God does not require them to stop being Black, or to conform to a standard set by White culture, but simply to be proud, respectful, and aware that their status as children of God informs how they should carry themselves.

They should exhibit respect for themselves and others, be responsible in their behavior, and considerate in their bearing and conduct. Peace, love, joy, patience, goodness, kindness, faithfulness, gentleness, and self-control are all fruits of the Holy Spirit, evidence of God's presence in one's life (Galatians 5:22-23). Behaving in a Christlike manner does not mean a surrender of one's culture.

Being peacemakers and resolvers of conflict is a big challenge for young people who grow up in the inner city. It is in direct conflict with the rule of the streets. But being a peacemaker does not rule out direct action, a fact to which civil rights protestors could attest. As an oppressed people for generations past, Black people have been both bold revolutionaries and ardent peacemakers, standing against injustice in the struggle for equality. We must help our young men to learn and take up this part of our culture in order to stand up for the weak and oppressed in our society. Our youth should be the harbingers of unity and peace in the body of Christ. In urban America, Black youth often are angered and enticed to violent response as a result of unfair treatment and abuse, in schools, by police, in the courts. Those who minister in these settings must help our youth find more constructive ways to address injustice than self-destructive anger. Black urban culture already greatly influences American society in fashion, style, music, and the arts in pervasive ways. The impact of Black spirituality on America must continue through the lives of our young people.

Black youth tend to applaud the rebels and violent protestors of our history against slavery, segregation, and injustice, identifying with righteous anger at injustice. I rejoiced in the movie *Black Panther*,[1] but there was one part I did not like. At the end, the antagonist Killmonger proclaims that he would rather die than receive grace from T'Challa; he says he'd rather be like his ancestors on slave ships who chose death over captivity. There's just one problem: if it wasn't for those ancestors who endured captivity, none of us American Blacks would be here today! Above all, our urban youth must come to a new way of thinking, of seeing themselves, not as simply victims of an unjust society. That old paradigm of self-destruction leads to death. These kids cannot be confined to how others perceive them: a society that is often scared of them or ignorant of their culture, but instead they must boldly live out their promise in Christ,

> **Young Black men must not succumb to the low expectations of others around them, at school, work, or other places, but instead strive to be all they can be with the confidence that comes from knowing their self-worth in Christ.**

not apologizing to anyone for who they are. They must not be separated from the light of God because of the darkness of society, of racist or unjust treatment. They cannot allow their own thinking to be clouded by the darkness of this world but rise above it. Nor should they give in to the temptation to do bad because that's what people in authority often expect from them. Young Black men must not succumb to the low expectations of others around them, at school, work, or other places, but instead strive to be all they can be with the confidence that comes from knowing their self-worth in Christ.

Young Black men must "change the former way of life" and "clothe [themselves] with the new person" (Ephesians 4:22-24); not condemn themselves by believing in negative stereotypes and assumptions about themselves, but embrace the discovery of who they are in Christ as strong, pure, holy people. They must embrace a new, God-given attitude with Christ as their model, which will allow them to approach the righteousness and holiness and practice the godliness that God requires. So they cannot resort to lying, stealing, and inappropriate behavior to express themselves. Bad character will not be accepted under the ruse of *acting Black*. We must teach them to be kind to everyone, be helpful, to do the most they can do in any situation, whether it is appreciated or not. This is what I learned growing up in a Black family. By doing all the good that they can do, tempering their anger, refusing to explode in destructive ways, young people will demonstrate that they are living for Christ to further the cause of Christ. By forgiving, though not forgetting historical and societal slights manifested in daily injustice and insults, drawing upon the presence and grace of God within, they will be divinely used by God as agents of change in the world.

FROM DARKNESS TO LIGHT

In following the example of Christ, not that of the world, we all must rise above the world's values, to essentially live on a higher plane than that of our surroundings, our peers, and broader society. My mother used to tell me that to succeed as a Black person in this world I had to be "better" than my White peers, that I would have to work twice as hard to be considered just as good. She was right. Throughout my life I was often overlooked, passed over, or ignored in school, social, and professional settings. But it made me want to work harder at school, be better at my job, be tougher in my mind; I wasn't going to let anyone devalue me. As ministers and leaders in underserved communities, we must encourage young people to be *better spiritually* too. We must be better in order to forgive past and current injustices and slights and move forward to make the world a better place. Simply being good by the world's standards won't cut it. The forces opposing Black people's success in life are too entrenched and formidable. To make it in this world, Black men and women need God's Spirit. It will be manifest in them if they can embrace who they are and live like God's people.

So keeping one's self pure is not just a good idea morally, physically, and socially, it is a spiritual imperative. Immoral sexual behavior as well as negative conduct has an impact on the spiritual well-being of Black men and women and impinges on their quality and prospects for life. Too often racism, poverty, and systemic injustice breed negative, self-destructive behavior by youth; but as the Church, the people of God, we must find this unacceptable and hold to the higher standard of Christ. In that way young people may emerge from the darkness of society's expectations into the light of freedom in Christ. God calls the young Black man to a higher existence in God, not only for himself, but in order to be a model and guide to others around him, even to the world. We must help all young people to embrace this calling, to be the people God wants them to be, seeking wisdom and understanding of God's will and their purpose in life. Along this path lies peace beyond understanding, overflowing joy, and abundant love.

CONCLUSION

Like Paul, who wrote the Book of Ephesians when he was in chains, young Black men are in bondage in underserved communities all over America.

But they can break the chains of poverty, racism, and injustice through the knowledge of who they are in Christ. As the Church, as the body of Christ, we must lead them into this knowledge. Instilling this fundamental sense of identity must be the focus of discipling young people, particularly African American boys. We must teach them that their strength is in the Lord and his mighty power. It requires a supernatural, spiritual strength to overcome the obstacles stacked against them. Because their enemy is not simply flesh and blood, not simply political, social, or economical, but the spirit of this age, which is contrary to God. So if they choose to stand with God, they will be a target to the world. They need the protection of the knowledge of God, because the day of evil has come, and they need to stand.

Urban young people have to be equipped spiritually to stand against oppression and despair. They must be able to stand, not just for themselves but for others as well. God equips them to stand through truthfulness and being true to God and self. They can stand before God and before the world as God's agent because the righteousness of God covers them through the blood of Jesus. The gospel that they spread through living their lives is one of peace and unity, not disharmony. They must protect themselves with the assurance that faith gives that they are on the side of right and that God is with them. Through this faith they will endure the insults, stings, and injuries perpetrated on them by an unjust society. Their salvation is assured in Christ, who can stand against them? Who need they fear? God accomplishes this through his Spirit. Young Black men should be men of prayer, constant and fervent, for themselves, each other, and for our world community to which they belong.

Eventually, our worst fears came to pass for Tyree. Over a period of months he hit a series of setbacks just as he could see the finish line at the end of the race. He had had a run-in with the police and although he was exonerated in court, he had lost his job. He couldn't pay rent so he lost his apartment and was sleeping in his car. He couldn't make the tuition payment for his final semester at school, so he could not finish his degree. As a result of failing to meet some technicality, his baby mama got the court to remove his custody rights to his son. This crushed him. Tyree had finally lost hope. He told me he was going to do whatever it took to get money, so he could get his child back. "I know how to get money in these streets, Chris!" was what he told me. For weeks I didn't hear from him or see him. I feared the worst.

But one day he called and said, "Guess what, Chris?" Somehow, he had found a good job, with benefits. In addition, the college had found money to pay for his final semester's tuition. He was living with his mom, from whom he had been estranged. He was going to court with legal aid to reinstitute visiting rights with his son. Against all odds and expectations, he was all right. He didn't turn to the streets for what he needed, he turned to God. He prayed and hung on after months of struggle and suffering, trusting God to bring him through. I don't have to worry about Tyree; he has learned that God is there for him. Not every story ends this way, but I know that in Christ, young Black men in the hood can find meaning and fulfillment in life. God will bring them through the shadows they face. God has not forsaken them. God will bring them home.

My prayer for Tyree and others, adapted from Ephesians 3:16-19 (NIV), is:

> *"Out of God's glorious riches may God strengthen them with power through his Spirit in their inner being, so that Christ may dwell in their hearts through faith. And I pray that they, being rooted and grounded in love, may have power, together with all the Lord's holy people, to grasp how wide and long and high and deep is the love of Christ, and to know that this love surpasses knowledge, that they may be filled to the measure of all the fullness of God."*

LEADER GUIDE

LEADER GUIDE

INTRODUCTION
FOR LEADERS

This leader guide will help you use this book, *Not Forsaken: Growing Up Black, Male, and Christian in the Hood*, as a study resource for group Bible studies. *Not Forsaken* examines the issues facing young Black Christian men in urban communities, providing a resource for youth workers or anyone who works with young urban Black men in a Christian context. This leader guide is designed to help leaders in forming and conducting Bible studies with their kids, in their unique setting. Its components include

- an introduction describing the purpose of the guide;
- practical suggestions for setting up your study sessions;
- nuts-and-bolts details on how to run your sessions;
- instructions on how to use the DVD that accompanies the leader guide;
- eight study sessions that may be used to lead a group of youth in the *Not Forsaken* study.

There are also free Bible study sessions for youth, available for download at https://www.abingdonpress.com/notforsaken, which the youth may work on individually or take home for private use.

I wrote the book as a vehicle to share my experience of working with Black male youth—boys and teenagers, in inner-city Minneapolis for thirty years. I have attended many conferences and seminars over the years, but the most valuable aid that assisted me in my work was to just do it. The most valuable teacher has been the Holy Spirit, through experience. We've all been in places when we've felt inadequate and discouraged, but the challenge before us is to trust God and work out the issues and problems we are confronted with through the guidance of the Holy Spirit. There is no substitute for you and God working it out. My book is the result of God and me working out the problem together of "How do I reach these kids?" Advice, training, and support are valuable, but none of these can supplant the presence of the Holy Spirit in your life and ministry.

My hope is that through this book you draw inspiration for your own journey and setting. I hope that you see similarities between some of the situations I describe and those of your ministry, and you can gain insight that will help you minister in your community. I hope the knowledge that someone else went through this and God helped him to figure it out will help you commit to your path and focus on finding a way to illuminate your own community with the light of Christ.

SETTING UP YOUR SESSIONS

Choosing Your Group

Your group of youth should be kids you are already in relationship with. These studies are not designed for evangelism or presenting the gospel to unbelievers. They target young men who have been exposed to the gospel and have become Christians but need guidance on living the Christian life, particularly in the urban context—in short, discipleship. The kids you want are those who already have a connection with each other; church youth group, a basketball team, a group of friends, or a group that has shared a camp experience together. You want to have a group of kids who are comfortable being open with each other and with you.

You want to have a small group as opposed to large. You want to encourage discussion and active participation by everyone, and this will happen more readily with a small group. One leader with six to eight kids maximum would be ideal, and of course you may conduct more than one group. Kids who know each other and are friends or share a bond are best together. You want to engender a sense of trust in the group.

Choosing a Place

For your meeting place you want someplace that is first easy to access and get to for everyone. It should be a place where everyone feels comfortable. It cannot be in an area that is known for having associations with a particular gang, for example. It must be a neutral site where all feel safe. A church is an ideal place. The coach or the youth worker's home would be good. It should be a place where there are no distractions and affords some privacy and little interruption. Ideally it should also be a place that has access to positive diversions (game room, gym, and so on) as an incentive to participation. Being able to have food or snacks is a must. Gotta feed your kids!

Choosing a Time

Choose a natural time to meet with your kids. By that I mean a time when they would come together anyway. Like at the gym or church or possibly even school. If your boys gather for practice of any sports or activity, that would be a good time. If your church or agency runs an after-school program, it could occur then. It would be OK to have them gather specifically for Bible study, but I've found it easier to get regular participation if I partner Bible study with some activity they enjoy doing like playing in the gym or even playing video games. And yes, I use food as an incentive. Instead of a formal weekly meeting you could have regular overnights at church or youth "lockdowns" at the gym and make your study a part of that event. Adding incentives for completing the program is a good idea as well, such as a special event or activity for participants who complete the series.

RUNNING YOUR SESSIONS

Typically Bible studies have two primary purposes. The first is to gain biblical knowledge. The purpose of biblical knowledge is to increase one's knowledge of God, thereby discerning his will. This type of Bible study presupposes the desire of participants to grow in the knowledge of Christ. Evangelism is not its main aim, nor is it directed toward unbelievers. The primary goal is to share and gain information, to dissect the biblical material and ingest information for spiritual gain and insight.

The second purpose of Bible study is to help participants to live the Christian life. To learn practical applications that will help them in their pursuit of discipleship. This kind of Bible study is like a nuts-and-bolts, "how-to" discourse. It presupposes that the participant wants to be a follower of Christ. Typically these Bible studies are topical, exploring pertinent life issues, learning biblical principles, and learning how to apply them. Participants want to know what God requires and how it can be manifest in their lives.

The Bible studies in this guide have elements of both of these objectives. But while they accomplish the first objective of dispensing biblical knowledge, their main focus is on the second objective of practical application of biblical truths in youth's lives. Your target audience is urban young Black men, and this study is tailored specifically with their needs and struggles in mind. The goal is to provide Christian Black male youth with a manual for negotiating life as a Christian in an urban context.

The studies that follow may be used in a variety of ways. The leader may use them as a lesson plan for running a session. Or the leader may copy each session (or give out the downloadable sheets) so each participant has one in hand and they work through them together as a group. The leader may also copy sessions and distribute them to youth to do at home and then meet once a week to do each session as a group.

However the leader decides to use the material, here is a rundown of each of the components:

- Introduction
- Discussion
- Scripture Study

- Reflection
- Conclusion
- Prayer

Gather Kids: Bring your kids together in the area you've chosen to meet. Allow some time for dialogue and playfulness . . . hopefully this will be a group that is glad to see each other. At the first gathering, after the initial greetings, explain the purpose of the group and why you have brought them together. Allow time for questions and comments. This is a good time to provide snacks before serious discussion begins.

Introduction (Let's go!): Each study begins with an icebreaker leading into the topic you will be working on that session. If there is something you come up with that fits your group, that would be ideal. Be sure to supply any materials needed.

Discussion (Chop it up!): The study sessions come with questions designed to elicit group discussion and individual participation. The discussion will delve deeper into the topic of the study and the leader should be careful to listen so that he may discern what the kids are thinking and feeling about this matter. You want to hear their opinions. Ask the question, then give time for youth to respond. In order to break the ice, you may share your own personal response, or call on someone you know is comfortable beginning. Let the conversation go where it will, but be prepared to maneuver it back into the direction of the study itself.

Scripture Study (What does God say?): What does the Bible say about this subject? At this point in the study the group will read the scriptures provided. The scriptures will reveal what the Bible says about the subject at hand. Having thoroughly discussed the subject, the group will now examine what God has to say about it and how that compares with individual opinions and society's stance as well. Sometimes a scripture's meaning may be clear to all, sometimes not. Allow for each person to wrestle with the scripture and discover its meaning for themselves.

Reflection (Think about it): The goal is for youth to think about their lives, and how the scriptural truths you've discussed may apply to them.

141

The studies are designed for youth to express their opinions and thought in their own words and in their own way. Anything goes as far as youth expression, as long as it is not abusive to others or self. Some kids will be ready and willing to talk and share right away, while for others it will take time for them to feel comfortable doing that in this setting. It's OK to sit and think about what has been said, or to call for a few minutes of silence to pause and think and consider. Take time and make allowances for each individual to move at his own pace.

Conclusion (I'm down with Christ): Each session will end with a challenge, or call to response. Outline the difference between what God says and what society/culture dictates on the given issue. Delineate the choice between following God or following the world (or one's own way). Discuss the consequences of the choice. Stress the fact that if one wants to be a disciple, a follower of Christ, one must go God's way. The point of this part of the meeting is not to elicit a specific response or require that a certain choice be made, but to make the choices and options clear so that each person might make an informed choice, in his own time.

Prayer (Chop it up with God!): Close the meeting with prayer. Ask each person to offer up a one-sentence prayer. Each session ends with a prayer suggestion that the group may offer, which summarizes the main idea of that session. Pray for your group and their families. Pray for the community and their schools. Pray that God helps them to be the men he wants them to be.

Although the structure for these sessions is laid out, I encourage the leader to first familiarize yourself with the subject, then make it your own. The strength of your effectively communicating the truths of the gospel to your youth lies in your ability to be real with them—not "hip" or "cool," but real. Be you. Do you. Your youth will respect this and listen to what you have to say. Trying to be something you are not leads to mistrust and doubt, barriers to trust and effective discipleship.

The material I've provided is meant to be a guide. Take and use what works for you and don't feel like you have to follow the lessons verbatim. When I do studies with my guys, my goal is to communicate and share one basic idea or concept. Scripture and my own life experiences are tools to do this, but what really seals the deal is my relationship with my youth. I don't even call our time together "Bible studies" but refer to them as mentoring or leadership sessions. Learn what works in your setting and go with it.

Be relaxed, be comfortable, be you. I like to tell stories so I make storytelling a part of my sessions. Maybe you like drawing or some other art form, music, dance . . . technology, YouTube videos, online stuff . . . whatever your personal likes are, infuse them into your time with the kids. Let them see who you are. Prayerfully invoke God's presence and allow God to work through you and your relationship with the kids. Because it's not by might or power, nor by polished program or impressive study guide, but by God's Spirit that hearts and lives are changed!

USING THE VIDEOS

Not Forsaken is meant to be a resource for urban youth workers in their work. In this accompanying DVD are a series of videos crafted to introduce each section of the study series.

Introduction (for leaders). In this video I share my motivations, challenges, and joys over thirty years of doing ministry. I briefly discuss principles that I have learned through my years of doing youth ministry in inner-city Minneapolis. My prayer is that my experience may be a source of inspiration and confidence for you—inspiration through the Holy Spirit and confidence in the Spirit of God working within you.

Session 1: Images of Christ. This video presents your youth with a series of images of Christ as a person of color. Use it to spark conversation about the novelty of seeing Christ this way. Discuss its legitimacy. Replay as often as you need to for them to get the full effect. Use their conversation as a springboard into the Bible study.

Session 2: Man Up. Here is an example of me and my group of boys hashing out the issue of growing to manhood. The themes of "what is a man" and "how do you know when you are one" are addressed by the youth. Use their responses as a springboard to in-depth discussion in your group.

Session 3: A Godly Man. (There is no video for this session.)

Session 4: Christian in My Context. This piece flashes common sentiments and statements on the screen that I have heard young Black men make in my experience of doing ministry. They refer to the difficulties and obstacles faced by young people who choose to live a Christian life in an un-Christian setting. Watch the video with your group and ask them if any of these statements resonate with them, or if they can add new ones.

Session 5: Just Wanna Be Happy. The young men in the video discuss what gives them happiness in life. Although they touch on a lot of things—family, people, helping others, being successful, justice—they keep coming back to having purpose in their lives. In this study, lead your kids in a discovery about what God says about finding their own purpose in life.

Session 6: How Do I Fit In? This video shows stark images of the disconnect and fear facing many young Black men. The expressions and feelings shown by the young man in the video are intense. Question your group about these images to see what feelings they evoke among them. Don't be afraid of difficult or intense emotions. Allow the boys to express how they truly feel and comfort them through prayer.

Session 7: What Does It Mean to Be Black? In the video, the group responds to the question, "What does it mean to be Black?" They address many aspects of being Black but they keep coming back to the theme of power, strength, and confidence. The concept of resilience captures all of those qualities. Resilience: the ability to adapt to and recover from adversity, stress, or trauma. Our young Black men need resilience to get through their daily struggles in order to survive and thrive in today's world. In this study stress the importance of resilience to your group.

Session 8: Who I Am in Christ. You will need to play this video repeatedly so that your group can listen intently and pick out various themes that are addressed. The themes include:

- self-condemnation, not feeling as if you measure up to God's standard;
- personal fallibility and the commitment to grow;
- the question: "What is God's plan/purpose for me?";
- the assurance of Christ's belief in you, and your ensured success.

Examine these themes with your group assuring that self-doubt is OK, but faith in Christ is what assures our growth as Christians.

SESSION ONE

IMAGES OF CHRIST

What color is God? For young Black men who often feel like they have no place in mainstream society, this is an important question. The traditional image of Christ as a White man is neither relevant to their culture nor historically accurate. Although many Christians and churches profess themselves to be "color-blind," the reality is that in our society race matters, and for urban youth it is critical. It is important to ask this question because it needs to be pointed out that although God has no color per se (one could say God is all colors), he is the author of all ethnicities. All "color" comes from God. The focus of this study is on the ability of Black youth to connect with God, and to identify with Christ. This is a step in the process of discovering who they are in Christ as a Black person.

Introduction: Let's go!

Watch the video, "Images of Christ."

- Did you see yourself in the images of Christ? In what way?
- How do you feel seeing Christ portrayed this way?

145

- How important is it that Jesus "looks like you"?
- Different ethnic groups portray Christ in different ways. Why?
- Do you relate to these images? Why?

Scripture Study: What does God say about it?

John was a disciple of Jesus and a close friend.
Read about his vision of Christ in Revelation 1:12-16.

- How does his description compare with other images that you have seen?
- Consider the phrases, hair like "wool" and feet "like burnished bronze" (NRSV). Does this sound like a White or Black person to you? Why?
- Do you think it matters what a person thinks God or Jesus looks like? Why?
- If Jesus came to your neighborhood, and he wanted to fit in with everyone else, what would he look like?
- What would he wear? How would he act?
- How would you know it was Jesus? How would you react to him?

Read John 4:24: "God is spirit, and it is necessary to worship God in spirit and truth."

- What do you think this verse means?

The Bible says that God is spirit, and therefore has no human body, color, or ethnicity like we do. He is beyond those things. But for the present, in our society, color and culture have a significant impact on our lives. God has no color, yet all ethnic groups come from him. So the question "What color is God?" is not about his physical appearance; it has to do with how we identify with him, how we relate to him. Different cultures portray Christ in different ways to reflect their own cultural identity. What color is God to you?

Reflection: Think about it!

Can a Black person relate to Jesus? Do you feel like you can relate to him?

Discussion: Chop it up!

Young Black men in the city may find many points of identification with Christ.

Read and then discuss the following scriptures.

Matthew 2:13-18

Like young Black men in the city, *Jesus was endangered as a child*. After the wise men from the East came to visit Jesus as a child, King Herod tried to kill him. King Herod actually murdered an entire community of male children two years old and younger in order to get Jesus. But Jesus escaped because God warned his father to take his family to Egypt.

Luke 2:22-24

Like many young Black men in the city, *Jesus grew up poor*. He was born in very humble circumstances and it is obvious Mary and Joseph were not wealthy (born in a stable). According to religious law the firstborn male must be dedicated to the Lord through an offering of a pair of doves or pigeons. But in the Book of Leviticus (12:8) we see that the law requires an offering of a lamb. And only if you could not afford a lamb, pigeons or doves were acceptable. If one needed pigeons or doves you only had to go out into the desert and catch one. This is the offering Mary and Joseph made for Jesus.

Luke 2:41-52

Like many young Black men in the city, *Jesus was likely raised by a single mom*. The Bible mentions his father, Joseph, up until Jesus was about twelve, but when Jesus is an adult his father is no longer in the picture. At least for a time, there was no father in Jesus's home.

Matthew 5:38-42

Like young Black men in the city, *Jesus was persecuted and harassed for his ethnicity*. He experienced racism as a Jew in Roman-occupied Judea. Jesus's admonition to turn the other cheek, surrender your cloak, or carry another's burden derives from the mistreatment Jewish citizens received from Roman soldiers.

Like young Black men in the city, *Jesus's lineage made him Black.* We know that Jesus was born and raised in a part of the world whose population was a blend of African and Asian forebears. By the "one drop" Jim Crow–rule of segregated America, if you have one drop of Black blood, society considers you a Black person. By our standards today, Jesus was indeed a Black man.

Conclusion: I'm down with Christ!

- What are some ways that you, as a young Black man, may relate to Christ?
- What are some things you have in common with Jesus?

Prayer: Chop it up with God!

Lord, help me to realize that you made me, you know me, and you have plans for me. You made me how I am, and I am a wonderful and special creation. I can relate to you, because I come from you. Help me to know that I am special, because I come from you; in Jesus's name. Amen.

SESSION TWO

MAN UP

Negative images of Black manhood abound in the neighborhood, the news, and TV shows. Kids are subjected to negative stereotypes about Black manhood in society and in their own communities. Stereotypical roles such as athlete and entertainer are what enthrall popular culture, but what does it mean to be a Black man? The path to manhood for many boys in the city lies in the streets. Boys must learn that there are other ways for a Black man to be successful besides what they see on the streets, hear in rap lyrics, or see on TV. They are not bound by negative stereotypes or popular ones either. They must look inside themselves, and turn to the Creator, to discover the true path to manhood.

Introduction: Let's go!

Watch the video, "Man Up."

- What did you think of their discussion?
- Were there any questions or responses that you especially liked? Any that you disagree with? Anything you would add?

149

Scripture Study: What does God say about it?

Read 1 Corinthians 13:11: "When I was a child, I used to speak like a child, reason like a child, think like a child. But now that I have become a man, I've put an end to childish things."

- How do you know when you become a man?
- What are some of the "ways of childhood" that you must put behind you?
- What are some ways men talk, think, and reason differently than boys?
- Name some changes boys go through toward becoming a man.
- Name some things you will be able to do as you grow older: when you are sixteen; when you are eighteen; when you are twenty-one.

Reflection: Think about it!

- How do you *know* when you are a man?

Discussion: Chop it up!

The Bible offers a formula for growth from Jesus's life.

Luke 2:52: "Jesus matured in wisdom and years, and in favor with God and with people."

Wisdom: A young Black man must have wisdom. The pursuit of knowledge is critical to thrive in society today. But along with knowledge the young Black man must learn to use and apply it. European (White) culture thrives on academic knowledge, but the nature of African (Black) culture derives from experiential, practical, and relational knowledge as well. The young Black man in American society needs knowledge from both cultures. Working hard to gain knowledge and training at school and submitting to authority over him (parents, teachers, employers, police) is the path to wisdom.

- What are some ways you can gain wisdom?

Stature: A young Black man must be healthy in mind, body, and spirit. The body is not just about the physical, but we must seek and possess emotional health as well. Being physically and emotionally fit in our practices and daily habits is essential. Avoiding any form of chemical abuse (drug) or dysfunctional attachments (abusive relationships), having healthy lifestyles and positive relationships make us strong.

- How can you grow in stature?

Favor with God: A young Black man must grow spiritually. He must be connected to God to be authentically Black. We only gain God's favor if we honor his Son and submit our lives to him. Our relationship with God through Christ is the most important one in our lives. Our identity must be in Christ.

- What are some ways you can grow spiritually?

Favor with people: The young Black man is a part of society and as such must gain favor with society. We have to give respect in order to gain respect. No one will respect us if we do not respect ourselves. If we are strong and positive on the inside, we will reflect those attributes on the outside. We are leaders and great contributors to society, not outcasts and castoffs.

- How can you gain or earn respect from others?

Conclusion: I'm down with Christ!

Instead of looking to others to signify when you have reached manhood, young Black men must turn to God.

- What kind of man do you want to be? Describe this person.

Prayer: Chop it up with God!

Lord, help me to find my path in life. Help me to be the man you created me to be; in Jesus's name. Amen.

SESSION THREE
A GODLY MAN

It takes God to be a Black man. The source of our pride and acknowledgment as Black people resides in our Creator God. This is the anthem young Black men must carry today if they want to break out of inner-city bondage. Prejudicial attitudes often view Black young men in the city as being criminal, lazy, and untrustworthy. Even among their peers and families, negative and self-destructive behavior is often accepted as part of "being Black." Our youth must be taught what being Black truly means: strength, spirituality, and positivity. God is the source and strength of a Black man. Facing circumstances of urban, social, and moral decay in their lives every day, urban Black male youth must be equipped to rise above their circumstances to pursue lives that are spiritually strong and pure. The main idea of this study is to teach youth to look at Christ as the model of godliness and manliness.

Introduction: Let's go!

Play a game of "Hangman" with the boys, first using the word *respect*, then using *responsibility*.

The two Rs of manhood: respect and responsibility!

Respect

A Black man craves respect, but it must begin with the self. You cannot expect respect from others unless you have respect for yourself. People can tell if you have respect for yourself by the way you conduct yourself and the way you treat others. Being respectful to someone, even if you are angry, is not about submissiveness. It's about inner strength. You gotta give respect to get respect!

Responsibility

The main thing in life an adult man has to do is to be able to take care of himself and those he loves. This is his responsibility. Being a man is not about being tough or strong physically, it's about being responsible—in your job, at school, and especially in your family and relationships. We learn responsibility by taking on responsibility. If we fail and fall, we have to pick ourselves up, dust ourselves off, and try again.

Scripture Study: What does God say about it?

Read Galatians 5:22-23. These are the attributes of a godly man, the fruits of the Spirit: peace, love, joy, patience, self-control, kindness, goodness, gentleness, faithfulness.

If you want to be a godly man, then you will follow Jesus and try to live like him. The fruits of the Spirit are qualities that grow in you as you try to live for Christ. They are opposites of ungodly, or worldly, values.

Read Galatians 5:19-21 (NIV). These are the attributes of a man far from God, the acts of the flesh: sexual immorality, dissensions (arguments and separation), impurity and debauchery, factions (gangs), idolatry and witchcraft, envy, hatred, drunkenness, discord, orgies (wild parties), jealousy, selfish ambition, fits of rage (uncontrollable anger).

- Give examples of the qualities from both lists.
- Which list is more common in your community, the acts of the flesh or the fruits of the Spirit? Tell some instances of when you've witnessed these attributes in your community.

153

Reflection: Think about it!

- Which kind of man do you want to be?

Discussion: Chop it up!

Situational ethics are a morality, or sense of what is right, that is dictated by the person and circumstance: they change depending on the situation.

For instance, many people think it is acceptable to lie, cheat, or steal, even kill to survive. Do you? Explain.

Which would you do? [You have to choose one extreme, you can't be in the middle.]

- Smoke an offered joint?
  Or refuse and be called a goody-goody?

- Steal something from a store?
  Or do without something you really want?

- Beat somebody up to take their shoes?
  Or keep wearing your "busted-out" ones?

- Have sex with a girl?
  Or have people call you a virgin?

- Work a job where you have to clean bathrooms and wash dishes?
  Or be broke?

- Cheat on a test?
  Or study and do your best?

- Start a fight at school?
  Or have people call you a punk?

Many people think doing wrong things are acceptable to get ahead. What do you think?

Are there times when doing something wrong or unlawful is acceptable behavior? If so, describe such a situation.

Conclusion: I'm down with Christ!

- What would it take for you to be a godly man, or Christian?
- Can you name any behaviors or sin that is keeping you from being a godly man?

Everyone has to choose. Do you want to be a good, or godly, man, or do you want to be an ungodly man? If you choose to follow Christ and live out his values it will not be easy, but it will be rewarding, both for this life and the one after. Choose what kind of man you want to be. Surrender your sins and ungodly desires to God; then through Christ, God will help you to be a new person. If you allow Christ to work in you and change you then you will be a godly person, a true Black man. None of us can do it without Christ.

Prayer: Chop it up with God!

Lord, help me to be a Christian. Help me choose to follow you; in Jesus's name. Amen.

SESSION FOUR
CHRISTIAN IN MY CONTEXT

What does it mean to be a Christian in the hood? A young Black male's self-image is shaped by the influences of home, school, and peers, the most influential group being that of his peers. A strong family bond may offset this, but in terms of time and influence, peers and popular culture have the most impact. The peer group is the predominant source of community for urban Black male youth, influencing values, dress, conduct, and choices. It is critical for a young person to choose friends carefully, surrounding themselves with people with similar values and goals in life. The home is another setting that has great hold over how a young person views life. The circumstances of family and the home environment define a young person's outlook on life and how the world is seen. If family life is positive, it's all good. But if family life is hard, one must overcome it to be the person one wants to be. It fundamentally impacts how a young person views and interacts with the world and broader society. It is crucial for the young urban male to orient himself according to the strongest moral compass he may find, that which he finds in Christ. Building identity in Christ equips the Black male teen with the self-image and esteem necessary to overcome the emotional and social perils of life in the city.

Introduction: Let's go!

Watch the video, "Christian in My Context."

How relevant are these statements to your life? Rate them on a scale of one to five, one being irrelevant and five being very relevant.

- "I have to do this [something wrong/illegal] to survive."
- "I struggle to make good choices."
- "I'm afraid to become a Christian."
- "I have to protect my little brother and sister from the streets."
- "I have to protect my mother from her boyfriend."
- "You have to know whose turf you're on [or you're liable to get jumped]."
- "You have to be hard [to make it in my neighborhood]."

Explain your responses.

As a Christian in the city, you are often in conflict with the accepted social values of those around you. In the hood you have to live by a code of "street wisdom," and sometimes, to live like a moral Christian is to invite abuse and disrespect.

Scripture Study: What does God say about it?

Read Matthew 16:24-27. This is what Jesus said about being a Christian, a follower of Christ.

"All who want to come after me must say no to themselves" (v. 24 CEB) or "deny themselves" (v. 24 NRSV): this means to put aside the things you want in order to do the things Christ wants you to do.

- What is a "something" you have to stop doing, to follow Christ?

"Take up their cross": this means to follow Christ's example. The cross was the method by which Christ died. To take up the cross means to surrender our own lives to be the person God wants us to be.

- What are some things in your life you may have to give up to be more like Christ?

"And follow me": to follow Christ is to be obedient to his teachings.

Read Hebrews 13:5-6: "*I will never leave you or abandon you.*" If you give your life to Christ, he will be with you to help you—always—even in the hood.

You are never alone and you do not have to be afraid, because God is with you!

Discussion: Chop it up!

There are many dynamics in the inner city that make it difficult for young Black men to live a godly life. The presence of gangs, crime, street violence, police abuse, domestic violence, and drugs breed fear, pride, greed, racial discrimination, and sexual temptation.

- How can these things keep a person from following Jesus?
- What makes a Christian different from anyone else? How does a Christian act?

What did Jesus say? Read John 13:34-35.

- Is it difficult to live the Christian life among your peers? If so, why?
- What about at home?
- Have you ever been in a situation where the behavior expected of you by your family was in conflict with how a Christian behaves? Describe the situation.

Reflection: Think about it!

- It's not easy to follow Christ. So why should you do it?

Conclusion: I'm down with Christ!

So in the midst of the unique struggles facing you as a young Black man in the city, God calls you to be a follower of Christ. To live right, to have integrity, and to follow his teachings. He does not say it will be easy, but with God's help, are you up for the challenge?

Read 2 Corinthians 5:17: "If anyone is in Christ, that person is part of the new creation."

If we surrender our lives to Christ, he will help us be the person he wants us to be.

Prayer: Chop it up with God!

Lord, help me to surrender my life to you, help me to make good choices and live the way you want me to; in Jesus's name. Amen.

SESSION FIVE

JUST WANNA
BE HAPPY

Happiness is experiencing personal satisfaction and fulfillment with one's life and circumstances. But happiness eludes many urban Black male teens caught in cycles of dysfunction and abuse beyond their control. It's easier to go along with the flow of your life than to break out of intergenerational cycles of dysfunction—of poverty, chemical abuse, gangs, and crime. Young Black men in the city today need a sense of hope that things can change for them.

My mother always told me what she wanted for my life was for me to be happy and content, and for me to be able to take care of myself and my loved ones. She didn't care if I became rich or famous, but she wanted me to have security and fulfillment in life.

The secret to true satisfaction and fulfillment comes through relationship with God through Christ. The peace, security, and fulfillment that communion with God yields are beyond this world. The only path to this joy is through obedience to God. This is the path of hope.

160

Hope is that spiritual quality that enables one to experience peace and fulfillment in the midst of the most trying circumstances. Hope leads to joy and happiness. The object of this lesson is for our youth to know that they can be happy, in Christ.

Introduction: Let's go!

Watch the first part of the video, "Just Wanna Be Happy."

- When asked what would make them happy many of them referred to finding purpose for their life. What do you think they meant by that?
- What is your purpose in life?

Scripture Study: What does God say about it?

What is the meaning of life? The writer of the Book of Ecclesiastes asks this question. This guy was rich and young; he had everything you might want, but he did not have a sense of fulfillment. He needed purpose in life, so he went to find it. We see in the first two chapters of Ecclesiastes he tries everything. Wisdom, pleasure, work.

He tried knowledge and wisdom. He studied everything. He says he was the smartest guy around, but yet he wasn't happy. Today he would've been a scientist or a doctor. He would've had the respect of everyone. He would've written a bunch of books. He might've been a professor or started a library. He must've been the most important person in his world, but he did not find fulfillment or purpose.

He tried pleasure—doing stuff that makes you feel good. Anything that could make you feel good, he did, but it didn't give him satisfaction. Partying, getting drunk, using drugs, having sex with a bunch of different girls, all kinds of things that give people momentary pleasure and make your body feel good—but he was miserable.

He must've been very wealthy. This guy built houses and buildings and all kinds of enterprises and big projects. He was large and in charge, very powerful. He bought a lot of stuff, trying to be happy. In today's terms he probably had houses, cars, game systems, clothes, you name it. But he didn't find fulfillment. He says, "When I observed all that happens under the sun, I realized that everything is pointless, a chasing after wind" (Ecclesiastes 1:14).

"Everything is pointless," he says, nothing matters (Ecclesiastes 1:2). He tried to discover the meaning of life through wisdom, pleasure, and power, but it only made him empty and miserable.

A lot of times we think money will solve all of our problems, but it doesn't. It didn't for him!

We all need purpose in life. Purpose gives us a sense of fulfillment. Fulfillment is that which makes you happy and content.

- What gives you satisfaction in life? What makes you feel content or happy?
- Is it material things?

Read 1 Timothy 6:6-10.

You may have heard that the Bible says that money is the root of all evil, but what it actually says is that the *love* of money is the root of all evil (v. 10). We can extrapolate the meaning of this verse to say that it is not money itself, or possessions, that bring happiness to a person, but gaining a sense of satisfaction and peace. This is what makes a person happy. On the contrary, the Bible says that if we make those things our primary goal in life, it will bring us unhappiness.

Reflection: Think about it!

- Can money make you happy?

Discussion: Chop it up!

Unfortunately, the acquisition of wealth and material possessions is a prevailing characteristic of our American lifestyle. But this will not bring you contentment or happiness. Those of us who grow up in humble circumstances often fall into the trap of believing that being rich would solve all of our problems. That it would make us happy.

- Do you think a person can be happy in spite of living in difficult circumstances (for example, being poor or sick)? Explain.
- According to 1 Timothy 6:8, what does a person need to be content in life?

- Which would you choose: happiness and contentment, or wealth?
- Can a person have both? How?
- Which is more important to you?
- God's plan for you is to be happy, content, and at peace. Regardless of how much money you have or where you live.

Read Hebrews 13:5-6.

Remember, there is nothing wrong with wanting to be rich, but we cannot let our love of money or possessions come before God or other people. In life, you can gain long-lasting happiness and contentment, regardless of your circumstances, by living a life for Christ. If you have Christ, you have everything you need to be happy.

Conclusion: I'm down with Christ!

Read Ecclesiastes 3:12-14.

So the writer of Ecclesiastes discovered that the true meaning in life is to be happy and do good. This sounds too good to be true, too simple, but it's true. It's the way God made us.

We can find happiness in the things God has given us: family, relationships, our jobs, hobbies, and other things; and we can do good by helping others. This is how God made us. If we commit our lives to serving God and doing good, God will give us everything we need. He promised.

Philippians 4:19: "My God will meet your every need out of his riches in the glory that is found in Christ Jesus."

Now isn't that better than just being rich?

Prayer: Chop it up with God!

God, help me to be happy and do good in my life. Help me to accomplish the dreams you have given me; in Jesus's name. Amen.

SESSION SIX

HOW DO I FIT IN?

The need for belonging and community is critical, a basic need for all human beings. Urban Black youth are trying to find a way to fit in—in an environment that daily does damage to their self-concept. Sometimes the easiest and quickest avenues for acceptance are illegal or fraught with danger while positive avenues, the ones that require hard work and patience, are often frowned upon by peers or disregarded by family. In order to avoid trouble in the neighborhood one needs to be familiar with the ways of gangbangers, their wannabees and drug dealers, and others. Urban Black youth find themselves immersed in a culture of ghetto behavior whether they share those values or not. It is often hard for Black young men to find acceptance in their neighborhoods without engaging in negative behavior, but in living for Christ a person will find genuine community and belonging.

Introduction: Let's go!

Watch the video, "How Do I Fit In?"

Everyone has a basic human need to belong—to have a place where they feel like they fit in.

- Does the young man in this video feel like he has a place where he belongs? How can you tell?
- Do you ever feel that way?
- Do you have a place or places you fit in? family? friends? school? your neighborhood? other?

We all have a basic need to fit in, a need to belong. You can't survive without it. If it isn't met in positive ways, it will be met in negative ways.

- What are some negative ways your peers try to fit in?

These are often stereotypical behaviors young Black men in the inner city engage in to find a way to fit in. But you don't have to, because you belong to Christ.

Scripture Study: What does God say about it?

Read 1 Corinthians 3:21-23.

You belong to God! You don't have to follow someone else to feel like you fit in. You don't have to try to be like someone else to try to fit in. You don't have to do something you don't like or that you are not sure about in order to fit in. You are fine just the way you are. You belong to God!

Read Psalm 139:13-18.

God made you, and he made you special and unique. Take a moment and look at your fingers closely. See the pattern of swirling lines on your fingers? That is your fingerprint. You are the only one in the world with that print. There is no one else like you. No one else in the world has your unique DNA. When God made you he broke the mold!

- How does that make you feel about yourself?

Reflection: Think about it!

God made you special! You are one of a kind!

If you recognize that you belong to God, you are part of a special community, like a family. The community of God. The Bible calls it the Church, the body of Christ.

Read 1 Corinthians 12:12-26: The body of Christ is the Church.

- What is the main characteristic of this community?

Read Ephesians 2:19-22.

You are not a stranger who does not fit in. You belong to God's people. You are a part of God's family!

- In the video, there is an image of a police officer firing a gun. How does that make you feel?

There have been far too many instances of the police shooting young Black men in our urban neighborhoods. There are far too many instances of gang violence and shooting as well. It promotes a sense of fear and lack of safety among inner-city residents. Fear and the threat of violence is a fact of life for many young Black men.

- How do you live with it?
- What is the opposite of love?

If you said hate, you are wrong. The opposite of love is fear.

Read 1 John 4:15-18: "There is no fear in love, but perfect love drives out fear."

God is love, he is perfect love. If you are in God (living for God, loving God) you do not have to be afraid. You do not have to be controlled by fear or fearful things, because you belong to God. If you live your life to serve God and help others, even if you live in a dangerous environment, you don't have to live in fear. You can live in love. You can live in Christ.

Conclusion: I'm down with Christ!

The Church is any group of people who come together in Jesus's name. The Church can be your group of friends, your family, or your sports team.

If you share a connection to Christ, this is your family. This is where you belong, with God first and with others who belong to him. The Church is where you find belonging. The Church is where you find love. Whatever else you do in life, this is your essential connection. Your relationship with Christ is the most important relationship in your life. It gives the rest of your life meaning. If you know who you are in Christ, then you will know where you belong. No one can make you feel left out, no one can make you feel small, and no one can tempt you to do something that you know is not right. You are a child of God!

Prayer: Chop it up with God!

Thank you, Lord, that my life has meaning because I belong to you; in Jesus's name. Amen.

SESSION SEVEN

WHAT DOES IT MEAN TO BE BLACK?

In many American cities most of the Black population (if not all), is found in the center-city neighborhoods—typically low-income areas. However, the experience of Black people in urban America today makes up a just a part of the whole that is the Black experience, historically and in modern times as well. Our youth must be provided with experiences and models of Blackness that extend beyond their immediate community. Young people who are insecure in their Blackness, or even ignorant of it, embrace negative stereotypes acted out around them. We want our young people to be secure in their Blackness: to embrace the richness of African American heritage, the strength of Black culture, and the deep spirituality of Black people. These things must be shared, learned, experienced, modeled, and felt by urban Black youth so that they have a sense of who they are and what it truly means to be Black. Knowing what it means to be Black will give urban youth inner resources that will allow them to survive and thrive growing up in the inner city.

Introduction: Let's go!

Watch the video, "What Does It Mean to Be Black?"

- What do you think of their responses?
- Anything you would add?

Reflection: Think about it!

- What does it mean to you to be Black?

Scripture Study: What does God say about it?

In the video the young men alluded to the power, strength, and confidence that come with being Black. One person pointed out that those qualities come from enduring pain and suffering. This is resilience, the ability to adapt to and overcome adversity. This is a critical part of our heritage and what it means to be Black—enduring suffering and struggle, building resilience to be strong and confident in pursuing our life goals. This resilience is what every Black person needs to succeed in life.

Read James 1:2-4. God uses suffering and trials in every person's life to bring us closer to God.

Read 1 Peter 3:17-18. Black people, like Jesus, have often suffered even though they have done nothing wrong. And because of it, we, too, may be made alive in the Spirit.

Blackness comes from God. God made us. God is the author of Blackness. The Bible tells us that everything God created is good (Genesis 1:31). So whatever else it is, being Black is good. Being Black can be difficult sometimes, a struggle, maybe even an inconvenience. Being Black can be a stumbling block to other people, but that is their problem, not yours. Our Blackness comes from God, and it is good.

Blackness is biblical. Some of the most influential people in the Bible are Black, or dark skinned, having come from Africa.

- Moses is one of the most important people in biblical history. He was the leader of his people whom God used to lead them out of slavery, and God used him to give the Israelites the laws and bring them to the Promised Land. And Moses was married to an African woman (Numbers 12:1).
- Simon of Cyrene, who carried Jesus's cross, was a Black man from Africa (Matthew 27:32).
- Some of the leaders of the first organized church in the Bible were from Africa (Acts 13:1—Simeon called Niger [the Black man], Lucius of Cyrene [in Africa]).

For that matter, most all of the people in the Bible, being in the ancient Near East, were people of color. Everyone in that region of the world was a mix of African and Asian cultures. Therefore, one could make the argument that most people in the Bible are Black.

Black people have a spiritual heritage. Enslaved Africans somehow discerned the truth of who God is from their hypocritical "Christian" masters, practicing and living out the gospel of Christ in a dehumanizing existence. Prayerfully waiting for deliverance while at the same time actively struggling toward their own freedom. This spirituality sustained them through emancipation and the subsequent Jim Crow era in which the dehumanizing of African descendants continued. This spirituality enabled them to take the higher road in the civil rights struggle that delivered civil freedoms although paid in blood. Black people must depend on that innate spirituality today as they continue to suffer from discrimination and racism resulting in disempowerment and poverty.

Conclusion: I'm down with Christ!

In order to not just survive but thrive in the world today, young people need resilience. Resilience is the ability to adapt to and recover from adversity, stress, or trauma. Young Black men can find resilience in Christ.

Through biblical teachings and their own cultural heritage they can find a strong moral code to guide them in life. Through identification with Jesus and trying to live for him, they can overcome the stress and pressures of prejudice and racism, which they may encounter at every level of society.

Being Black is good! Being Black means to be spiritual, connected to God, and trusting him to take care of you through the hard times. To be Black means to be strong, to endure through suffering. To be Black means to be moral, to do what is right, and to think of others before yourself.

Prayer: Chop it up with God!

Lord, thank you for making me who and what I am. Help me to honor you by being the best me I can; in Jesus's name. Amen.

SESSION EIGHT

WHO I AM
IN CHRIST

The goal of this study is to cultivate strong young Black men. Not young Black men with picture-perfect lives, not young Black men without any problems, not young Black men who are good all the time, and not young Black men who are perfect Christians, but young Black men who have hope, young Black men who trust in God no matter their current circumstances, young Black men who, when they fall on hard times, use their faith in God to pick themselves up and keep moving forward. It is the knowledge of who they are in Christ that will enable young Black men in the city to cope with any circumstance they find themselves in. For many of our Black youth, one mistake is all it takes to change the course of their lives. All it takes is one seemingly insurmountable problem to tempt them to give up and quit, but if they know who they are in Christ there is no doubt in their hearts that they will make it. Faith will help them get through the hard times. Not faith that they will be saved, but faith that God will help them achieve their goals in life. If young Black men learn who they are in Christ, they can overcome any obstacles to success and personal fulfillment.

Introduction: Let's go!

Listen to and watch the video, "Who I Am in Christ."

Listen to the poet and pick out the themes that touch you personally.

- What do you hear him saying?
- Is there anything that you identify with?

Being a Christian is all about faith. It's not about what you do, it's about what Christ did. It's all about your position in Christ. When Jesus died on the cross for us, he opened the way for us to be positioned in him as a child of God. It affects who we are in relation to God, in relation to the world, in relation to sin. If we are in the right position, nothing can move us. And that position is being in Christ. Knowing who you are in Christ gives the Christian advantage, strength, and power for life's struggles. It's a knowing that comes by faith.

Scripture Study: What does God say about it?

Read Ephesians chapter 1. Paul repeatedly speaks to the benefits and effects of being in Christ for the believer.

- Verse 4: In him we were chosen to be holy and blameless.
- Verse 7: In him we have redemption and forgiveness.
- Verses 11-12: In him we were chosen for the praise of his glory.
- Verse 13: We are included in Christ, marked "in him" for the promised Holy Spirit.

These things are ours simply by virtue of our position in Christ. The believer does not have to do anything to be forgiven, to be holy, to be chosen by God, to receive the Holy Spirit. It has already been done for us by Christ! We do not have to do anything but believe it and own it. We have not earned it—it is given us by God. We are saved by grace, through *faith*.

Grace means to incur God's favor. It cannot be earned, no one is good enough. We don't get God's grace because we are good, or because we go to church or because we don't do bad things. We receive it because, and only because, we believe in Jesus (faith). It is a gift from God.

You have been chosen by God. Not because you've earned it or deserve it in any way, but simply because he loves you. Describe how that makes you feel about yourself and your life.

Read Ephesians chapter 2.

- Verse 5: Instead of being dead in our sins we are alive with Christ.
- Verse 6: We are raised up with Christ and seated with Christ. [Where is Christ? At God's right hand, and we are with him.]
- Verse 10: We are created in Christ to do good works. We are on this earth for a reason.
- Verses 12-13: We were separate from Christ (spiritual death), but now by his blood we are in Christ.
- Verses 19-20: We are no longer strangers, but members of God's family, in Christ. We are not lost and alone, in Christ we belong!

Now how do these truths apply to the life of a young Black man living in the inner city? The young man who embraces this truth of being in Christ and internalizes it will revolutionize his life. He will never be the same. Nothing and no one may stand against him. No problem cannot be solved, no obstacle cannot be overcome, no person can hold him back, the devil cannot defeat him. God is for him, who can be against him (Romans 8:31)!

Discussion: Chop it up!

Ask the boys what their greatest struggle in life is right now.
Hold a brief time of prayer, asking God to help each one.

The main thing holding young Black men down in our society is not racism and prejudice. The main thing holding young Black men back from being the men they are created to be is the belief that we are subject to our circumstances. The belief that we have no control over our lives. **You have control over your life!**

174

Young Black men respond to problems in their family, problems at school, problems in their community, problems in society. We believe that our choices are limited by our problems, that we have no control over our lives. But we do! **You have control over your life!**

Many young Black men believe that the locus of control is external, that they are controlled by circumstances around them. It is not. It is our own choices that control our lives. The locus of control for young Black men is internal, not eternal. If you surrender your life to Christ's control, nothing can hold you back. **You have control over your life!**

In order to have success in life, young Black men have to shake off the shackles of seeing yourself how the world and society sees you. You have to see yourself how God sees you: as being strong, intelligent, capable, and full of promise and potential. You have a calling in life—to believe in Christ and to do good works! Giving Christ control of your life is accepting freedom to be the man God created you to be and rejecting the bondage of this world.

Conclusion: I'm down with Christ!

Being in Christ gives you purpose as a young Black man.

Being in Christ gives the young Black man community and a sense of belonging. Being in Christ gives the young Black man control over his circumstances and potential for his future. Being in Christ gives the young Black man power to be the person God wants him to be.

- Now that you know who you are in Christ, how is that going to make your life different?

Prayer: Chop it up with God!

Lord, help me to know who I am in Christ—that I am a child of God, that I belong to you. Help me to give my life to you completely so that you can have control of my life. Jesus, come into my life. Take over my life so I can be the man you want me to be; in Jesus's name. Amen.

175

NOTES

Introduction

1   "Near North Neighborhood Data," Minnesota Compass, http://www
      .mncompass.org/profiles/neighborhoods/minneapolis/near-north.

2   Elizabeth Shockman, "Report Ranks Minnesota Among Worst Achievement-
      Gap States," MPR News, October 14, 2019, https://www.mprnews.org/
      story/2019/10/14/mn-among-worst-achievementgap-states.

Chapter One: The Color of God

1   Robert L. Short, *The Gospel According to Peanuts* (Louisville, KY: Westminster
      John Knox Press, 2000), 124.

2   Tom Skinner, *How Black Is the Gospel: A Decisive and Truthful Message for
      Today's Revolution* (Philadelphia, PA: J. B. Lippincott Co., 1970; Washington, DC:
      Skinner Leadership Institute, 2016), 73–74. Citations refer to the 2016 edition.

3   Cain Hope Felder, "Out of Africa I Have Called My Son," in *The Other Side* 28,
      no. 2 (November/December 1992): 10.

4   *The Second Coming*, directed by Blair Underwood (Los Angeles, CA: Quiet
      Fury Productions, 1992).

5   United States Interagency Council on Homelessness, "Homelessness in
      America: Focus on Families with Children," September 2018, p. 3, https://
      www.usich.gov/resources/uploads/asset_library/Homeslessness_in_America
      _Families_with_Children.pdf.

6   Equal Justice Initiative, "Black Children Five Times More Likely Than White
      Youth to Be Incarcerated," September 14, 2017, https://eji.org/news/Black
      -children-five-times-more-likely-than-whites-to-be-incarcerated/.

7   "Criminal Justice Facts," The Sentencing Project, 2018, https://www.sentencing project.org/criminal-justice-facts/.

8   "NAACP Death Penalty Fact Sheet," NAACP, January 17, 2017, https://www .naacp.org/latest/naacp-death-penalty-fact-sheet/.

9   James H. Cone, *A Black Theology of Liberation*, Fortieth Anniversary Edition (Philadelphia, PA: J. B. Lippincott Co., 1970; Maryknoll, NY: Orbis Books, 2010), 67.

Chapter Two: Becoming a Man

1   Paul Davidson, "Jobs Report: Black Teen Unemployment Fell to 19.3 Percent in September, Lowest on Record," *USA Today*, October 5, 2018, https://www .usatoday.com/story/money/2018/10/05/jobs-report-black-teen -unemployment-lowest-record/1536572002/.

2   Erin Golden, MaryJo Webster, and Mila Koumpilova, "Minnesota Graduation Rates Hit New Record," *Star Tribune*, April 23, 2019, https://www.startribune .com/minnesota-graduation-rates-hit-new-record/508943002/.

3   "Report of The Sentencing Project to the United Nations Human Rights Committee Regarding Racial Disparities in the United States Criminal Justice System," The Sentencing Project, August 2013, p. 1, https://www .sentencingproject.org/wp-content/uploads/2015/12/Race-and-Justice-Shadow -Report-ICCPR.pdf.

4   "Poverty: Quick Facts," *The State of Working America*, Economic Policy Institute, http://www.stateofworkingamerica.org/fact-sheets/poverty/.

Chapter Three: A Godly Man

1   Howard Thurman, *Jesus and the Disinherited* (Nashville, TN: Abingdon Press, 1949), 72.

2   "Wesley's Four Resolutions," from *Journal of John Wesley*, https://www.ccel.org/ ccel/wesley/journal.vi.ii.xi.html.

Chapter Four: A Christian in the Hood

1   Gerald M. Streets, MD, "The Homicide Witness and Victimization; PTSD in Civilian Populations: A Literature Review," *Jefferson Journal of Psychiatry* 8, no. 1, article 12, p. 59, https://jdc.jefferson.edu/cgi/viewcontent.cgi?article =1240&context=jeffjpsychiatry.

2   Berkeley Breathed, *Berkeley Breathed's Outland: The Complete Library; Sunday Comics: 1989–1995*, ed. Scott Dunbier (San Diego, CA: IDW Publishing, 2012), 9-10-1989.

3   CBSNews.com Staff, "The Delinquents: A Spate of Rhino Killings," CBS News, August 22, 2000, https://www.cbsnews.com/news/the-delinquents/.

Chapter Five: Just Wanna Be Happy

1   Langston Hughes, *Poetry for Young People: Langston Hughes*, ed. David Roessel and Arnold Rampersad (New York: Scholastic, 2006), 44.

2   Jawanza Kunjufu, *Countering the Conspiracy to Destroy Black Boys*, 2nd ed. (Chicago: African American Images, 2005), 31–56.

3   Brandt Williams, "Black Men Getting Involved," Minnesota Public Radio, January 21, 2002, http://news.minnesota.publicradio.org/features/200201/21 _williamsb_aamen/.

4   Brandt Williams, "Black Men Getting Involved."

Chapter Seven: Fitting In

1   Jeff Guo, "America Has Locked Up So Many Black People It Has Warped Our Sense of Reality," *Washington Post*, February 28, 2016, https://www .washingtonpost.com/news/wonk/wp/2016/02/26/america-has-locked-up-so -many-black-people-it-has-warped-our-sense-of-reality/.

2   See Michelle Alexander, *The New Jim Crow: Mass Incarceration in the Age of Colorblindness* (New York: The New Press, 2010).

Chapter Eight: Being Black

1   "When white Americans who live in a 'stand your ground' state make self-defense claims in situations involving a black person's death, 36 percent are ruled justifiable homicides, Robert Spitzer, a professor of political science at the State University of New York, Cortland, said. When the situation is reversed and black Americans make self-defense claims in cases involving dead white people in these same states, just 3 percent see those deaths ruled justifiable homicides. That's the pattern in more than a decade of data." From Janell Ross, "Arbery Case Exemplifies Abuse of 'Stand Your Ground,' but the Damage Is Broad and Systemic," NBC News, May 26, 2020, https://www .nbcnews.com/news/nbcblk/arbery-case-exemplifies-abuse-stand-your -ground-damage-broad-systemic-n1212816.

Chapter Nine: In Christ

1   *Black Panther*, directed by Ryan Coogler (2018; Burbank, CA: Marvel Studios).

CPSIA information can be obtained
at www.ICGtesting.com
Printed in the USA
LVHW042124210121
677137LV00005B/5